DIARIO DI UN OTTOGENARIO

POEMA CON MÁS LÁGRIMAS QUE MANOS

☙

IVÁN ARGÜELLES

2020
LUNA BISONTE PRODS

DIARIO DI UN OTTOGENARIO

POEMA CON MÁS LÁGRIMAS QUE MANOS

© IVÁN ARGÜELLES 2020

Carissimae uxori:
Marilla, who has endured my lyrical eccentricities
all these decades

What bitter's love but yurning, what' sour lovemutch but
a bref burning till shee that drawes dothe smoake retourne?
James Joyce, *Finnegans Wake*

Cover and book design by C. Mehrl Bennett

ISBN: 9781938521669

https://www.lulu.com/spotlight/lunabisonteprods

LUNA BISONTE PRODS
137 Leland Ave.
Columbus OH 43214 USA

DIARIO DI UN OTTOGENARIO

POEMA CON MÁS LÁGRIMAS
  QUE MANOS

ojos oídos en las plumas
de mis abuelos , ancho
y ajeno como el gusano
del pensamiento despeinado
o la cabellera de pirámides ,
dedos de hierba cortada !
asunción de la virgen
de mala leche , poema
didáctico de hiel y canto :
para qué las alas de piedra
si el pie no tiene ventanas ?

i

THE Roman Empire has not stopped falling
after all these centuries one rotted timber
after another creaking swaying in the wind
dinner for termites and other vermin
and trapped in the hour called eternity
and covered with eons of dust blind statues
stagger gyrating in the puzzling circle of sleep
searching for the quarry of their birth
Montale Pound and Kavafis ! each a finger
desiccated points a way to rock fragments
inscriptions effaced by immemorial rains
a breeze lifts an effigy gravid with human conscience
swirling epitomes of historical incidents
dots chiseled on a fallen parian column
ciphers of indignation and false rutting
women once saffron with desire pass like shadows
through the gutted murals of the underground
faded painting of the *House of Mysteries*
rouge and belletto formerly so bright on lips
a pale aspirin dissolving moon barely outlined
in the cracked Etruscan mirror held by
a skeletal hand a wrist without a pulse
the lists of emperors and empresses so haughty
with complicated hair Byzantine darkly waving
drenched in the tempests of a single night at sea
nothing more than erasures on withered parchment
alone and inconstant nowhere near the Castalian source
I listen to an impossibly beautiful voice
Vivabiancaluna Biffi ! who invented opera
with her singing and violin
I want to marry her I want to embrace her
for a day only before sinking back
into the macaronic chronicles of a gone antiquity
sputtered letters vowels detached from sense
entire ledgers of broken consonants

language suspended from the world of thought
and thought itself poisoned at the root
by mind the ever errant trap of sophists
and sorrow that lasts despite the fallen seasons
despite the unending fall of Rome

ii

THE imponderable weight of the years
bedlam in a single ear-socket the whole
divested of gravity and pounding like hail
against summer's frail window and to wake
to still another day smothered in fear of *being*
only the losses left to count the irreducible
ingots in a liquid history of memory itself
the one by one who dwell isolated in huts
dabbling in various encyclopedias of knowledge
Etruscology or myth of Beauty in the northern
latitudes the enormous *et cetera* that makes
us feel full and residents of a noon more
like ether than light asking as always
whether the last day is here is it Ragnarök ?
traffic of shining motors driven by deities
the decibels of speed the harmonies and disunion
of all that seemed perfect once like grass
and the budding leaf and blossoms white
and roseate in the puerperal dawn of life
whatever caught the eye whatever moved
like silk against a wind becoming red and rich
tapestries of the mountain on the *other* side
and twilights coming home to catastrophe
what made it desirable to breathe
if there was only desiccation a muffled voice
a tonic accent and a vocabulary of vowels
littering the plangent Homeric shoreline ?
imponderable weight of the years

consulting a Baedeker to get to Sicily on time
or thrusting one knee forward into glass
and forgetting the other one is there at all
the sleep of insects and drills and ciphers
how does one get home ? how does the rain ?
what is the first thought after dying ?
how does the lettered hoof leave its print
in the air ?

iii

between the hypothesis of the rose
and the difficulty of its thorns
lies the danger of losing consciousness
thin and fragile a sheet of light
floats with one darkness above
and an even greater darkness below
so what the eye presumes to see
a static mobility of brightness
is nothing more illusory than a firefly
blinking on and off between the powders
and dust of its own immortality
wings in motion dazzling in sunrays
the dragonfly too suffers immortality
pinned to the deceitful memory of childhood
there is no other time no other lamp
than the present coruscating
against a kinetic screen propped up
in the theater of night where we sit
immobile for a moment only
before lapsing into sleep eternal
with a start we hear a voice
something like a spinning microchip
inserted in the false cavity of mind
a dream ? it was and nothing more

names flake away into iridescent &
silent conflagrations which are both
beginning and end of the universe
++++++++++++++++++++++++++++
or is it the untenanted white shirt
hanging in the doorway?

iv

we are close to the godhead
and it is irreversible
unpaired shoes that won't put on
and patter of the inconsequential
is the next life really the *afterlife* ?
can it be any better than this
without antecedent and full of enigma
leaf torn from voice finger lost in grass
is the inch more accurate than the light
that reveals it or greater than the mountain
that without light is a useless mass of black matter ?
we measure without wanting to the passage
of days into meters and volumes of sound
disparate and inaccurate digitizations
called memory the flicker and switch
of images of statues dredged from the sea
of horses whose feet are not meant to touch
the ever elusive surface the unfathomable depths
the so-called divinities aroused from their sleep
of stone and immemorial pitch whose reign is
darkness itself the terrible presentiment
at the bottom of the stairs
and mind ? what is more inaccurate than mind
play-acting and thrust using false pronouns
egos of clay and saffron depictions
which are mirages the trance moment

of falling from consciousness
edge and limit of whatever space defines
as the known universe of chaos
myth and metronome of a kabbalah
that has no rules of interpretation
man's vain attempt to surpass himself
mountain and light and drug overdose
and to lie there breathless
and to lie there deathless

v

feet buried somewhere in the flowerbed
could still hear the voice but not what it was saying
by the crumbling wall near the cistern
behind the memory of the house darkening
a shadowy figure in the opaque window
a hand as if to wave goodbye to the world
dun colored everything like hills without redemption
and if we are to start the study of the great
European languages and to distinguish
between darkness and dialect and dialect
and army and army and the other darkness
that gathers at the borders and summons night
hands left untended behind the willow tree
by the side of the remembered house
and of the languages learned and unlearned
by rote the winch and the mast and the turret
glimmering by sunset on the hillside
the way we used to get home reciting verbs
regular and irregular until darkness
took us by the knees and all but losing
consciousness the small lights of the adjectives
and the silhouette in the window a platonic idea
at best and a sure method for language learning

kneeling before the fading image
of the great ancestor and come evening finds us
returned to the small feet at the bottom of the page
and the introduction in Greek characters
and of course the little of mind white dappled pink
the petals fallen in the bowl and the enormous
conjecture of night something even more remote
the distance of the mountain in an idiom
incomprehensible but for the falling tone
an accent at the head of the chapter and
for so many lines down the hexameter dubious
in its meters the disciples startled from their dream
the Master ropes around his ankles and dust
in a flurry in clouds all over covering head
and shoulders and turning to look if the screen
were on right and the play-show flickering
dim and somnolent the actors' voices like
an impediment to knowledge and how the moon
ruddy in its sudden affliction seemed to beckon
buried the rest of the broken consonants
'neath the painted gravel and falling into a depth
the world's illusions vanishing in a music
secret as the dialects gone dead to history
in a whisper in a hush a murmur of leaves

vi

put aside some fine calico print for
who knows one day it's use will be
if a shadow makes rain and the suffixes
to unknown words like clouds threatening
the cloister where sleep drains at noon
the slower maps faintly burning turning
to sand to the shape of a library in heat
somewhere to the south of the large

wading pool with its memory of cities
often too great for a circumference and
drawn on a white chariot by four totally
white oxen caparisoned in pure silver
ornaments and pearly stones and their eyes
directed towards a point in the orient
a hilltop where shimmering a marble palace
fixes appointments for the gods some of whom
you don't know their names nor the part
of the Sudan which is their origin and moving
as a wave across an unknown mere into
a troubling matter the division of kingdoms
into halves and then into thirds the light
of poetry the refinement within of sound
the beautiful voice effacing sections of air
with its troubling and gorgeous reminder
of human frailty outside where gunshots
can occur the parking lot the maimed
automobiles the motors still running oily
and viscous contaminating the utter azure
and on the saffron shore opposite trees
yearning to extend what they know into
the heavens above unmapped and violent
in their instant of coming and going

  Viva la Poesía!
  small and entering the rain
  each sound is a syllable
  high the lesson redounds
  its purity is celestial
  its memory forever !
  april cruelty no one
  fools but endures
  as does the light
  it engenders

vii

are there clocks and clothes that we put on
shoes that shape the day places and stations
we do not know like silver flashes in the sun
how will this hour bend in fractions of eighty-eight
a sum of totals in reverse a slag heap a palindrome
logic in the spit we scorn an empire in the leaves
pulled down by gothic hoards invisible in
their relief and sounds never heard before
anchored to the stillness by the listing bay
how many are the waters we cannot bathe
and which exactly is the god of plumbing
who lathers rust in his tiny lexicon of lies
we'll never understand the where and why each
sleep wakes to a different day until comes the
minute we cannot count and the blindness
sewn into the sky's great eye all yellow
gathered at the hem and spreading inks afar
until even the mountain lessens in its violet hue
and cattle in immense herds go lost in the dun
make me no more to remember the many and
how they just disappeared the ones embraced
unknowingly in arms of nerveless down
softer than dark gravity the head now slumbers
in its stone and immemorial services attend
like last rites in the deafened hive a dream
of swarms and clouds striated purple through
and through the lace and ivory and everyday
polish that coats each passing thought and
failing all the distances we never reached
brought suddenly to grasses where we lie
how do all these things come about so soon
so swift we can never understand but doubt
legend and myth pyre and smoking realities
the *this* of *that* and the never was of memory

viii

passer-by stop and look at this flowering stone
half-erased its inscription once read *here lie*
the remains   but years as dust
have come and gone and orchestras of crickets
and fireflies and the dazzling domains of the gods
on high in their swirling clouds of summer heat
was this once a Greek or an Achaemenid or just
some stone-cutter's unfortunate son whom
the Furies designed to fit a pattern of mortality
pools and ponds and drooping willow branches
a month or two in the thought of salvation
security from nothing so the late spring fevers
must have snatched him out of some reverie
turned to rock after only a year which seems
like centuries counting the febrile days of months
out of sequence and to whomever he once belonged
aged parents or stunned royalty dumbfounded
in an excess of grief watching as invisible boats
ply the harbor waters of a vanished port
to make music of silence and dew and to shadow
the steps carved in crumbling ruins a masonry
of feelings the size of Egyptian tombs and puzzles
stop just a minute and ponder the imponderable
small blue flowers come into life by mid-morning
then by some unseen hand from the southern sands
plucked to adorn the fantastic ceiling of the Underworld
a swooning in the aulic notes only the dead can hear
unpainted marble extensions of a winding corridor
then names of souls in backward script and mirrors
where the eons of an insectary unwind blown
out of line like a faded silken cloth remnant
of the days when historians and mythographers
declined like nouns the lineage of divinities
yet could no more proceed beyond this flowering stone

lamenting the cruelty of a finger cut from the main
dear traveler in music no more muse but grieve
the fate you will someday share
a blade of grass pressed to the lips a whistle
lost in breezes that comb these archaic leaves

ix

readings from the lesson of history
turk versus *greek* in noisy sea combat
statue on the right noseless one hand gone
statue on the left hidden from memory
big empire and bigger hair on its empress
pleats and hems and slightest emotion
in acid footnotes is what I wake to
still another fray a day's worth of light
misgiven and grieving for the hour
that was determined in bull markets
and price fix and weary news reports
from the eastern front crumbling sand
libraries and museums shut for good
unification of the two germanies a hemisphere
at a time object of derision a ceremony
in wax and smoke the ribbon cutting
and the TV show about the cosmetologist
who became queen despite all odds
look for me in the Presidio this afternoon
begging like Socrates and if you can't
find me look amidst the trees the woven
foliage shadow mimicry and blossoms of
sunlight voices too small to understand
but alas you won't find me I'll be gone
to the crematorium to the harp concert
to the great pantomime of the souls
when all is deaf and done and the heights

to be reached no longer require distance
mummies get up and walk shaking hands
a tomb at a time and evening shivering
at its roots the enormous mountain of night
sudden and inky conclusion to the dream
with this burial of *greek* and *turk*
vowels that resound like suffused dusk
in the back room slowly winding down
as if nothing more could be written
and even less could be remembered
in the soundless book of time

x

which of the many have we been circling
the thought of an ideal city and setting
ourselves in the small circumference of a
radiance emanating from a still smaller lamp
the idea of life being a flawed convention
marking strophe and stanza with extravagances
of image and space and then coming back
to this noon this pause between circulating
heat and eternal cold the endlessness we
avoid by learning to read signs and ciphers
symbols of a tropical script a fever of illusions
topographies of Spanish and Hindustani ringing
chimes in the stifled airs of an afternoon as
always inaccurately remembered a quiz
of grass and leaf and by the roadside a stone
where to sit how to dissemble the fear aching
to make the hour stop go retrograde and sing
humming between bars of sleep and drugged
mornings painted in the early light of memory
spent and totemic moments wrapped like cellophane
around the bodies of the few deities remaining

the ones who sit on automobile hoods just
waiting for us to pass by to lure us with candy
with morphed waxes of beauty of cinematic
hallucinations yet just dross the foam and scum
of the glass of liquid immortality to make numb
to deafen to blind the inner eye to defect and
error the way the writing started then finished
in a loop hole of insanity saying the same things
over and over and being *high !* and striking
with a claw or hoof the atmospheres of mind
curlicues and daft signatures of ampersand
and asterisk all Greek superscript characters to
become tragic to wake at someone else's funeral
to recognize no one grieving and the kerchiefs and
somber hair and sky above pivoting out of joint
the black Aztec sun the immobile sphere of death
taking its pyramids and charades into the ant-heap
is it to want to sleep without wanting to *sleep* forever ?
you and then I each on the second step of a
stairway that will never be completed the utter
sadness OK you feel it too and we shake hands
a looseness of nerve come hold me it says in cuneiform
and if we could reckon everything by the sand
it takes to construct a library and only swoon
in the elbow of a hidden stream with its myth of
language and dragonfly and the music coming at us
swooping grand metathesis of drumrolls and
distance yes the finally and only thing remote
as the mountain of fairy tale and myth enigma
of all the words we could never fully understand
inscribed in the mirror's own backhand
muffled syllables antecedents to the mystery
that becoming multiple we will all become

xi

take me to where I have never been before
become for me a wing to live a breath and sigh
too many leaves to count to speak a language dead
and hands that beckon the far unseen and sounds
that echo in the shoulders' wake a frail entity
where I have never seen before the cliff resounding
high above the naked raft Ulysses plies undone
are there so many poems alone and then a final one
a section of marble and quoits of air and missives
written all in thumbs a bravado of recitations
some imperfections and lips of stone we yearn
take me to the ancient bluffs and azure palisades
a river around me wrap and put me deep to sleep
let mother come from her grave and feed me airs
that sing even though I will never hear come back
she says a mouth of continental silences rushing
through the grove where nymph and cicada abound
a wreathe and ghostly syllables and beauties infinite
worn like wristlets and ringing stanzas in the ear
never been like this before so take me one inch more
the night has only so many days before the hour
loses all control and minutes with their tiny shoes
go flying through a special hole into eternity's alphabet
drown and seize and strike to hurt the sleepless cavalcade
among them who am I and what clinic and hillside
and what memories in me reside that I cannot unearth
the tin and soldered alloy of a separate myth the mind
what marvels it unfolds speaking a hundred tongues
grammar and pencil of the evening shroud colorless
or many-hued the fingered cloud of dappled oblivion
wafts its sheets of lingering rope and tide and asterisks
at once advance on the tabloid sepulcher a host
of avatars and forgotten grasses shadows of the loss
we hold so dear the fragrances and soils pronounced

like vatic utterances in the rocky cleft of infinity
so take me higher to where I can breathe no more
and lapse like dew into a glass that has no other side
a cipher unraveling in the twin of space a lapse
and then to heights beyond the edge of time
take me to where I can be no more a shout as endless
as the moment before my life began

xii

it's time to wake John Lennon up
asleep about as long as he was alive
and the Roman Empire has come and gone
and punk bands and garbage flutes and hair
that wraps all around the Underworld
he's been washed by Apollo and scrubbed
by some sinister Egyptian deity and the girls
on the sidelines in their high school pinafores
the senior prom the outsize elephant parade
the drum-major who used a scalpel in the air
and the series of passing masks of love and hate
to wake John Lennon up and shout loud
into the vowel pronounced near his wounds
shot four times in the back as he entered
Priam's prize Trojan palace all jewels and dust
and the poets broke their lyres in despond
and as far off as Cipango courtesans loosened
their hair-pieces and snapped their combs in two
ivory pearl and musk the detritus of fame
and the experiment of art and the photographs
of unreason in a nightclub of pure alcohol
time to wake John Lennon and send him
to the river in the company of those Homeric twins
Sleep and Death and in the mirror of waters
let him see the fantasy of the world undone

newsprint and wrist-phones and abracadabra
writing backwards with smoke and shattered glass
the strange histories that go on without us
planets and suns with brand new orbits and voices
whispering nigh on these forty years
that death is not so bad that bullets have their songs
and mercury and venus have disappeared
and all the Billboard charts were wrong
imagine a Spaniard in the works
it's time to get up John and see all across
the universe how small space is in its drum
and how brief the instant between now and then
a writ in unheard notes a senseless syllable

imagine a Spaniard in the works

xiii

we all wanted to play like Elmore James once
I have put all that aside recalling George Harrison
who did play like Elmore James once but now
like all prophets wrapped as they say in the mists
of time has evolved into a mysterious figure straddling
the centuries wearing an alabaster white jacket
and walking mysteriously through groves
in an England beyond recitation of enormous
upended stone and legends of swords and lakes
prayer beads around his throat and a gorgeous
guitar slung over his shoulder and eyes set upon
an image of Krishna blue-skinned four-armed
chubby cute paraphernalia of the divine and
chanting praises as if they were a blues refrain
My Sweet Lord resounding in international airports
and small town bars alike the god-head once
so enigmatic now like a pop-song in reach
of the local nickel polished juke box and except

for the hints of plagiarism still sings loud within
the soul that many chambered palace of air
for if he has died we all have died living one
echo at a time in the boom-box of the post-modern
and no matter how skilled our fingers have become
cannot summon up as he once did the electric
and electrifying notes *While my guitar gently weeps*
sterile Sundays lost Mondays evacuated Tuesdays
the girl-singers hired to chime in at intervals
decided by a heavenly mandate like drizzle dissipate
outside a now vacant mansion in the London suburbs
an enormous birthday cake for the *Guru* waits
moldering and festering in the dead-eye of space
never again on a stage sounding like Elmore James
will George haunt us with his ethereal voice
we are admittedly grown old into our 9th decade
Joe has come and gone with his sun-letters and
moon-sounds chanting in his Gandhi uniform
that art is time and time is space and if only
but it all erodes in a single snap of the fingers
night turns in its request for stellar retirement
and George's voice a thin frail echo transparent
as cellophane sings

There'll come a time when most of us return here
Brought back by our desire to be a perfect entity
Living through a million years of crying
Until you've realized the Art of Dying

"Elmore James got nothin' on this, baby."

xiv

language can only go so far this afternoon
books and books and reading until the eye
looks for other Indias for other Gupta empires
for a persian alphabet just out of the kilns

for carpets and carvings chiseled in limestone
and inscriptions no one can ever decipher
mirrors and combs and artifacts useless to
even the deadest buried on the western slope
and how to hear the hissing sybil of the moon
anticipating the final form of speech as a
sequence of endings tagged on to spiral notes
vowels in proto-hittite and consonants devoured
in the murky dusk of a Pharaonic Mexico !
ants cockroaches and tribes of killer bees
building in their satanic silence pyramids of sleep
searching the leftover sky of the book's last page
and the poet who never used the right pronoun
addressing the *Goddess* discovers the almagest
and corrodes silver with his wasted mnemonics
and sings in a voice beyond the sonic scales
enough of bewildering grammar of syntax sewn
to eyelids of drowsing rishsis and cannibals who
demand their share of semantics and downgrade
the elemental basics of phonology rapturous and sad
both the grieving of the cocktail hour and the tempest
overlooked in the small vocables employed by
banal versifiers in their three minute epidemic
at the microphone the uncherished and loud
experiences and then the curtain and its dense
homophone the black sun of night and whatever
else the decision to remain human to endure
but language can only go so far and the shadowy
intent of the Homeric seas and the religions of
tree and stone and the most ancient of silences
mountain and sand alike and sleep when night
surrenders its insects of light and purpose
then does memory unfold wordlessly the child
who never asked for birthright nor the laws
of speech and meaning but sought some comfort

in the aphasic syllable in the unheard *Note*
punctuations of consciousness before dying

language can only go so far

XV

the interruptions the common feet an animal
beyond relief the life of hospitals and men
of crosiers broken unevenly and skies that
part between the hours and rains unending
in the believing eye how easily a second passes
into the day of infinity taking mint lozenges
and clouds and sparkling childhoods from
their lawns and terraces there are above
where deities hoot and weep watching below
the scalloped landscape of man's mind go
sharp against the reefs and how much remains
lost more than a tongue can say the suchness
of inarticulate suspense with its tiny alarms
wound up to nerve-wracking heights and
chariots brought to the door to sweep away
bodies that have never been and loud the saint
and louder still the bard locked in his chains
of sound and verb alas how much confusion
and dust and grasses torn by the roots a writ
held up to glass and people in a circle gathered
to cry and plead the noon of ghost and wing
mail from the university of heaven emptiness
insane locution lessons babble of inferno
ovens and sessions with Homer and Eluard
virtuoso schemes for memory sketched hard
against the brick and fusion and fission in space
and arrows that are love's messengers and
dying yes in even smaller doses a wedding and
its gift of hair unkempt Oh such a wreck to dive

where water used to be and reflect the silver
sheen of faces that cannot return and stone
too restless to sleep and sand burning to fly
each antiquity of the letter *Mu* is the start
of another mystery each ending of the copula
is the middle of a text without words and this
is why and this is really why I write this poem
and send it to all who are captured in recall
for whom the cinema of love's divided atom
destroys daily the will to breathe
a hand a leaf a spear of grass
and the finger too
alone

xvi
(a vision)

newly found in the *Avesta reader* instructions
for drinking *Haoma* for poets and priests especially
the new light the leaf that illumines the day
that never dawns tangled mysteries and romance
that begin in ancient Ctesiphon a mangle of dust
and enduring stone archways leading to grief
the capital of sorrow the endless strife between
dark and the forces of unending fire the flames
that sprout on incandescent but barren hilltops
where words and names in a language before memory
persist like the desiccated husks of insect tombs
I have been to these fields and slopes in sleep
and dedicated to the empress *Blanchefleur* the fever
of my adolescence and drunk deep of the *Haoma*
and thinking to start life anew stumbling over
vowels and consonants in the direction of East
mountains where summers circulate in a tempest
of bees and hallucinations map cities spread
over imagined meadows toward a Vedic summit

blind ! everything and everyone *blind !* in babble
and surfeit of whispers and the dying in tents
by the hundred who have warred unwittingly
and in the center the monumental *ego* of stone
painted like a sinister black sun or phallus and
swarming of *mind* trying to wake from the sundered
hemisphere of its birth and talents of gold and
edges of silver foil and immense ovens where writing
originates and the poets I among them a vision
more like the opaque histories of sand than breath
how came I to this step of the dream to this small
flare like a cigarette burning on the moon and
to speak to learn to talk in the vast parapets of
shadow hovering like cliffs over the Pharaonic lip
here in this instant all is a concentration of circles
wheels yet to be invented and horses of pure oil
swart and sleek stampeding on a solar syllable
how am I to find a way out of this maze of pills
and mescal and suicides writing love letters
with their plangent wrists and glass and steam
making of the sky an enormous asbestos sheet
white hot and in the shape of cows at evening
when it is time to return to the dark stables
and lay the weary head down to everlasting sleep
a music of one-string harps and sistra and planets
evolving out of a single fist held high in the sign of
Enigma all of space going out like a hissing thought
through the tiny ladder where I stand wavering
between age and the vanishing of mythology
grasses come running to take my feet and knees
the child I was the child I knew the child who died
all of them in me the absent lamp the declining
noun the final turning of the leaf at sunset
when like everything else I sink into a pool
profound as the ink of oblivion

xvii

in the reverse order of things we die
before we are born and an invisible hand
guides us into the painted palace which is
error of human conscience and if the body
is buried in the mountain and the seven stars
wash their hair in immortal light then can we
come down from our headstone and re-write
the cryptic dates the duration of a life
and if the comet comes burning its eye into
the screen where the pantomime of the souls
goes on into deep night of stone and leaf
with what do we regard the new dawn if not
as lamps put out to sea in their small red flux
and glassware placed carefully in the corners
what is that howling beseeching a return
underground to find nestled in her white shell
Persephone no greater than the number two
if the cause of things be eliminated and jealousy
and contrivance become paramount what becomes
of what we call the world and its thousands of
languages that are no more than a hair line
and the reeling in of the seas and the hoisting
high into the milky way the remnant of time
left to us numbering backwards the days to
the origin and the bone laid upon the rock
as if by that to read the intention to overcome
these last days who will know when darkness
comes and sleep shifts between door and door
being dead before arrival and hands once counted
for their ecstasies now lying immobile on cloth
colored with hues from the other side and in
her small voice Persephone calls yearning to feel
the green shoots rising against slanted sunrays
a morning as mysterious as any for resurrection

the rivers rushing in the opposite direction
and who will take from the husk the good seed
and who will remember to name what day
Osiris will come forth a dazzle and blind
between shadow and shadow the loss

xviii

what wet but staggers words these and
fish formed electricity the mind blows
shelves of water through loops a circular
thought to begin after ends the translation
to heaven a man's a grass a dew stain on
eternity filmed dark the night of insects
glitter flows porches reefer and struck
by down the gravid air its own light fails
eaten by coral and stinted disregard until
hueless the vast blank domain stretching sky
in azure cars fluidly archaic ram through
ink's unblended ramparts a rumor or a
gospel lesson about afternoons undeclined
a black more board than mind prepares a
sewn unstitched her eyelid's gown and flame
a bright that dazzles underscore it's death
of music that's most profound who sings
anthems or declare the poor soul we left
behind not knowing his why was up his
lung was lost and leafy entrance was just
parades away from the x-rayed doll in tears
lawns of distance and sooner than planets
circling their own void the immensity goes
doom floundered in the gassy seas of time

xix
Ragnarök

where exactly the universe is may be up there
in the northwest quadrant of chaos somewhere
outside of space the gods that rampant gamboling
like stars flecked and wounded by spears of light
underneath where zeroes multiply inside envelopes
the princely gear the eastward shoreline the dazzle
of comets stillborn in the riptide's flank a whiz
a whoosh the elevator shoes and parrying with
paper swords the gear of language a syllable
at a time using only vocatives and imperatives
hymn the glorious deities horse and chariot
fourfold without wheels the speed of melting
butter worlds collide evacuations of the mind
in a syntax of crag and boar the medieval ships
made from solid rock cleft and puppetry of color
design the innate text of embroidery and torment
talking in between loops of dwarf and miasma
tragic interlude where man defies man and
sings dying clouds and baffle of the mystic well
here lies unrepentant the monarch of mice and flies
Baldr of the black sun mistletoe and mayweed in battle
bandages undone sleeping sheaves of unbound wheat
local devices to turn the faucets off hands running
amok sleeveless the dangerous vocable at the wrist
appeals to cosmologists to reveal the shape of music
and heard swearing profusely in his ink the Thor
of glaciers doping and loud in ramshackle motel
some hybrid Nanna at his knee and hills and hollows
running west to scour the land for a burial spot
a place to inter the former universe a maze of cities
named after distant giants dysfunction and blot
of Gnosticism spreading through enigmatic grasses
clots of vowels in midair moons doubled and trebled

in a breath's notice and don't forget the primer
reprinted in Old Icelandic foretold of yore disaster
in ice and heavy shifts of red the kind that lacks
edge and margin and trumpet vines dripping blue
come the acid dawn and immense seas with spurs
running to take back earth and its evolving sounds
a lingering fate a remoteness of beds and capacities
for chair and mirror reflecting back an unknown universe
like the Christ of thorns angel inside a woman who
of fire makes dew into a single cosmic drop

xx

daybreak the frost of dreams scatters we age
imperceptibly until one day the window refuses
to open the shuttered fiction of light betrayed
unseen the lone ticky bird relentless in its one note
piercing the wan hour when everything runs out
sheets of thin ice lie over sheets of thin ice *the mind*
periphery of lakes hoary with distance and bamboo
talking in the russet winds from the east and hills
devouring themselves and the catatonic sky hanging
like a perpetual mist over the eye leaning against
its lamp projecting dim valleys of shadow lingering
atrocious memories of the rock at road's midpoint
do not pass remove hands isolate feet and nerve-ends
what is to come in a lesson that is more squiggles
than sense and the words washed in their own lack
stand separate from the sounds they represent
echo of the ear buried in a plethora of archaic vowels
sound shifts hues ranging between blank and blanch
the queen of the may reduced to a diacritic on
a page beyond interpretation lunations of longing
envy and subterfuge the human condition assayed
within a vast and inchoate parenthesis of breath

do we take another step or test the lintel once
more and oil the valves and administer last rites
to the grass lying still in the rush of darkness
that takes us by the knees and we reel falling again
on to floorboards of the sea and listen for the sirens
shapes of women who cannot disentangle themselves
from sleep and the metamorphosis of ink
when we can no more and write with a single finger
the dissent and the descent into great unknowing
illegible star patterns vanishing leaves dust

xxi

when only the photograph remains and not reality
not the body nor matter on either side of the universe
but the floral imprint on the retina echoes of hues
reiterated in a poetry of memory lost in dun hills
in the captured light the intact becomes dissolved
whatever time seemed to have been a pinprick
in the unevolving carpet of space spreading ever
farther from the reach of sense a density of void
only the photograph in its cold emphasis of form
contours that deny growth of shadow decrease
of light a havoc of chaos both sweet and ineluctable
wordless deformations of imprisoned spectra
that were once an essence a movement of features
a loudness and the surrounding silence of joy
euphoria of a summer spent in a single dewdrop
grasses and lichen and beckoning leaves voices
of the departed who escape like air from balloons
can one put an ear to the photograph to hear thoughts
whispered by the expired breath atoms of enigma
surprise of oracular discovery on the very edge
planets devoured in creation's fiery instant
and ink seeping from the shape of unending sleep

the more one looks the more it fades transient
as are all things in the useless traffic of perception
hullabaloo and grief in the moment of reprise
Big Bang ! click of the shutter all souls flee !

xxii
the last photo of us together
not have the final rapprochement though we walk
streets crowded with vowels and a lack of syllables
the marmoreal entrance to thought and its dictionary
a lapse of afternoons in a summer of conjunctions
the left hand and its lesson of versifying heights
a nosebleed a shadowy walk with nuns into the nave
candles spent and incense wafting in clouds the shape
of demons or imps from the Rg Veda and if there
is a right hand still functioning as a guide to the per-
plexed to the ignominious of memory walking avenues
shaded by months of porphyry did we not have
a final epistle a trajectory beyond the daily baptism
and crucifixion something on the other side of words
a chaos of invention in sound and ink with books
of uncut pages and leaves alphabetized for their color
and formation and the eye we shared like the ear
between the two of us which heard symphonies of utter
stone a pre-history of sand and the enormous fictions
of space with its eerie evenings without water and
what if we did say goodbye too soon and the buildings
curving around a Jerusalem of despond taking photos
with windows and reflections of a black Toltec sun
spinning its x-rays around our cinemascope brains
childhoods and childhoods we spent together like a
pair of unwanted Buddhas lying in an early spring
ditch more totem than idol more idiom than dialect
spans between thumb and index finger we aimed

our maps at the futility of language knowing full well
the birthright of platitudes and the silence of glass
crystalline dawns made static by our secret radio
oracular division of the number without quantity
what a mistake the bride was what an error the phone
and making up for a miscalculation in years we met
or so it seemed in a darkness of light outside the chance
that for the last time we would pose for the camera
of entelechy bright with the expectation of a future
grounded in the birth of our past a death beyond
reconciliation a loss of the eye and ear we shared
from the inception in snows and bitter melancholy
the famous *dot dot dot* of a code flashed from out
there hermeneutics and mandala of twin-speech

if we did say goodbye too soon

xxiii

which is the most if not the golden triangle
the marmoreal *mahals* I don't wonder
that this stuff is crazy with a reflecting pool
and dancing peahens and their own thunder clouds
purple beam the harsh setting on the hill
a sun as distant as a canker in may the jungle
of thoughts lattice-worked in the mind's eye
to predict the next demise of emperor and his
crown a size too big and Krishna himself
glory-robed in a long felt leopard skin
the trains at rest puffing their bellies steam
the wrought iron pavilion and flower-shower
heaped on the passing *rani* a mile below
milk-white steed and ornamental head-gear
millimeters of thick unkempt her hands aloft
blank gloves and a carillon for a voice bell-like
singing the mourning cry of the apostles

to make of this sense and painting backwards
across the tightly tilted Urdu characters a spell
in the world's oldest summer vagabond *rishis*
humming distraught to recall what comes first
dust or spark ? and standing on one leg for eons
living on breath alone black *anima* hotel
a thousand and eight rooms to be exact and
I don't wonder that it was difficult to get out
the temperature breaking records and stunned
in their pagodas and turbans the orientalists
Indra is king of the gods shouting in a lather
the furtive vowels the elusive ghats the parasols
made from human eyelids and the naked sahdus
eating orange goop cross-legged in waters
preaching which are the consonants to use
and which to eschew chanting holy and nasal
a backdrop of mountains where vowels
are copied and sent winging toward Bactria
shafts and a history of alluring beasts pasted
like damaged feathers to the backside of lotus
frangipani lesions moon blossoms of acid
asbestos aching to disburden the grief
that dwells within and the solitary ego
in a trance with its own hagiography
threads of light and the enormous Om
Devotion ! the ants who own the *masjid* and
bees swarming forever at the feet of the Beloved
sufi waistline ghazals intimacies of the Tavern
the hour of the Diwan orthography of noon
when the seas come rushing to adore
the dark knees of the formless god

xxiv

sumer is icumen in

mid-april now has death finished his first watch
grow brighter the dawn's opening flares and
shout from deep within the heart's chorus is glee
sky enjoys shifts between rain and darkness
shoots green and tender the opening salvos
unnamed beneath memory of snow small buds
to flower in the echo of vowels perennial gracing
branches that embrace awkwardly Zephyrus
come loosen clods and dig below earth's surface
white armed Persephone just inches from glare
strains to liberate herself from the hexameters
that have bound her underfoot to the dark House
have tossed seed carelessly and wood and beast
alike in the sun and the pyramids of thought now
wake the mortal groaning from a dream of loss
it's towards noon of ranunculus and hyacinth
to portals of water fresh sprung from a god's
locks the hoary brow the refrains of *IO IO !*
in spurts and spasms new breath from ink born
words more archaic than stone accents and tones
heaven spreads its azure sheets to whiten midday
yet nets still hold back the fish of consciousness
blacker steeds monumental with glistening sweat
break forth from constraints and reins plunging
with their red chariot into the western hill
to remind of the brevity of the casual hour
that has measured from birth man's paltry age
we go from room to designed room marveling
at the arts and reflections of the moving hand
histories pass from the unturned page and tales
and footnotes and scholiasts of the inexplicable
mid-april and yet do shadows hold sway and
the heavy circumflex of curtained futures

life and death seem equal life and death apart
birdsong and the unheard Note a *harp !*
from oblivion there is no retreat and light
the sum of all days seems as small and counted
as Persephone's short stay on earth *a song*

xxv

history of lightning and the circular narrative
of the waters in a thumbnail sketch of the skies
devastated repeatedly by a few carefully uttered
syllables the clash of arms and darkness so
casually buried in a blade of grass rhythm of vowels
unpronounced cascading in the drum's wild ear
where a single vibrating word carries at least
four thousand and eight meanings none of which
can be spelled correctly and noon its eternal heat
winding round and round lotus bifurcations
of torment and dangers implicit in the waking
sun with its orthographies of void and turmoil
matter heaped on matter like meat at day's end
stuttering and hissing of thought a section
at a time cut to the marrow and halved drained
by sleep's enigma cloistered dreams of rain
no greater than the primordial seed of sound at
the start of a lunar eclipse of the mind raving
for its content runaway planets the unequivocal
assembly of horses gathered on the tip of a flame
imminent birth and demise of language carved
in a stone of air emblazoned by an hour of clouds
minutes of non-existence fragments of echo given
over to a reading of the grimoire summoning angels
like homophones tumbling out of a postage stamp
engravings of geminated consonants in an eyelid
and to speak in this verbatim magnum of pyramids !

dancing asterisks heaped grains of jasper and jade
anemones pleading release from opium seas
mythology of words assassinated by nocturnes
failed representation of meaning and syntax
in the somnolent glare of the death after death
removal and hypothesis of sand brick by brick
recording jazz in the plunging taxi cab of time
it's all there in the hallucinatory moment of *truth*
chaos and harmony music and silence like metal
hurtling at speeds too infinite to comprehend
as much as the human aches to know too soon
lights go out walls topple dust resumes memory
of the dream *shadows not men*

xxvi

*el mayor delito del hombre es haber nacido
Calderón de la Barca*

on the east the gods reside ever hungry and keen
and to the south the ancestors and all other dead
from the north come the ragged generations of men
but leaning westward where sun lays his head
only mystery and the shadow of mystery
of what is space made if not the loom of sleep
hallucination and madness rust and silver
or simply the unexpected and inexplicable passing
of beauty and mind erased by the dusty finger
of the deity of *Transcending* and whatever illusions
remain whatever delusions and trance and mirage
wherever hospitals are blueprinted off the highway
and wherever bridges span unwanted waters and
the skies witless and splendid seem to unfurl
like spotted carpets or ink uncontained and restless
a loss of language the misuse of words a panoply
of adjectives derived from a silent catastrophe

somewhere in the archaic rock carving that persists
in the schizophrenic memory of the unnamed historian
who invented childhood among the innumerable suffixes
that haunt the cliffs hills and mountains of Cilicia
I couldn't see it coming ! and the banging and weeping
screen doors opening and shutting at midnight
and glow-worms and even tinier phosphorescence
of a subconscious alphabet and when the intimate
relationship between grass and fingers is revealed
and the grief at the end of the street by the cement mixer
and trying to recollect why mother sent us out
into the brief but intense noon of the hallowed seas
shining like bronze at the bottom of the well
if we could but remember to unwind the toys
fix misshaped shadows on the walls the imagination
that has created the oracular geographies of enigma
but *No* , we'll never understand nor why it had to rain
that night when the telephone came into being
with its multiple voices of bee and antler and the long
passage through the beckoning leaf through sounds
of soil and the slow erosion of earth in its cave
out there near the western fringe of time
where body and soul come together and fall apart
instantaneously in the *eye* that sees
but is not seen

xxvii

I could not see any farther within
lifting the great aridity of time into inks
depth laid over depth and porous rock
that defines afternoons in a schoolyard
light in alternating shifts dominating
and diminishing across the ethers and tempers
of a summer language punctuated in July

by the monosyllabic *jarchas* of the crickets
puzzling and intimate the interrupted memories
of the sea within the sea and in between them
the even greater waters of history erased
by a single shell roseate as an infant's ear
what was the enormous sound within saying ?
whence the thunder divided in two by a finger
and the clouds racing to their own origins
boxed in by a circle of heat and fierce
whatever was demanded of the Muse inarticulate
a savage month without Fridays a syllable
put to the lips of crocus or hyacinth to hear
their own monoliths repeated like evenings
inside a leaf darkening and without memory
of light nor of the race of days to their own
conclusion in the fuse of stone where
red gets even redder pulled by a thread
grieve no more ! the plaintive instance
issuing like a tiny crystal alphabet
and laid out to dry on the western slope
the place where shadows return looking for
some trace of what they once owned

xxviii

my brain is a maze of recycled echoes !
summers more ancient than stone
and the many grasses small and rushing around
reciting rapidly all the verses of the Rg Veda
is there anybody lying next to me sleeping loam
atavistic skies wrinkled from too much bleach
can I read Plato in the dark ?
which tree is the one that divides life from death
and at the apogee of the cloud that has just
entered my eye a cliff full of the letter Chi !

we must be getting ready for the trip
to Minneapolis to see where Hiawatha falls
and there is a tower in the distance so high
it goes half way to paradise and back and rumbling
in the ground are the tom-toms and mosquitoes
the fervent ants playing their marimbas
and so much else aphonic and deafening
to sleep with all this and the recycled echoes
to live forever in the beautiful capital of Grief!
tomorrow I am going to throw all the books away
tired of complicated orthographies and homophones
texts restructured to enable the blind to feel
the countless vowels unable to relax with so many
stories epics tales of the other side of the heavens
where people like Apollo and Gandhi have it out
too much and so little time left to breathe
give me a leaf with nothing at all written on it
tear the phones off the walls
I can't stand hearing all these tiny clusters
of mouths reminding me who they once were
I have a sister and a wife and as many empty rooms
after July what happens next ?
there is a deep black sun in my heart
there is something that won't leave me alone
that breaks my siesta into three hemispheres
molten pearl seas of Homeric noon !
and yet and yet and yet this chill
my broken ships ! my thirty and a half horses
my wild runaway and forever lost horses

my brain is a maze of recycled echoes !

xxix

all that is empty because the sunrise
and the jewelry of the stars fading effigies

gods at every turn of the way and climbing
steps and stringing pearls with their teeth
and gods who do not reckon in human years
and isolation the moon sewn together out of
melancholy and other faces coming and going
which is the alternate sky the vehicle bright
as heated clouds and the essence in between
the covers and the pages of a diminished text
like grass worn around the temples and the
altars still smoking from the last sacrifice
the mortal effort to get out of the skin
to simply forget what the other day brought
high blood pressure and the rusting lawn mower
attitudes about the ego and its brothers
drugged hours in the faded continent nostalgia
brooding within the darker elements sown
by an errant wind and the mountain aware
of its own collapse by the side of a schism
who will never comprehend and the password
abruptly denied the visuals and the wall
where display the planets their loss
circumflex and elliptic and forces beyond
language that is empty by sunset long trilogies
of light unwound and the skin like a song
passing from view the syllabic entries
to the other world the underside of time
throbbing at the pulse and small voices like
birds inside their shells a moment too late
and the words that define emptiness the ravines
crevices in the brow short-sightedness to hold on
as even water falls from its shape and night
the motion of fire the silences erupting out
of the vocalic subdivisions in an oracular text
stone and the summer of stone and heat
edges of time limits to space hands groping

for the feel of anything at all in the failing
breath instinct to paint what remains of the void
a fierce carmine a vanishing flash of red
seas incarnadine islands last seen going over
the margin of smoke and horizons duplicated
in the raving eye of the seer left behind
rock and sand and maelstrom whirlwinds
the ear and then sleeping the plangent weeds
glass that lacks exterior and flames
that fuel the speeding chariot into sunset
empty as the oncoming thought
of death

xxx

the secret is in the trees
in the small dark voices of the leaves
there is no fortune or history only echoes
silence plows no ground and skies burn
if bidden before dawn and my dead
my counted and my uncounted dead
each a whisper each a blade of grass
there is nothing coming back once red
has been shot into the hills and language
the polyphony of wind and pebbles
is reduced to the imitation of grazing
deep within the ear's drowned sea
oracular faces of pre-meditation !
landfalls and guises of eternity in the stone
that slowly opens its mouth to the dew
blind alphabets come pouring out of
the statue like the waters of genesis
walls begin their archaic threnody
behind them the abyss of sulfur and laurel
and the mountain that is a running wound

when is a word ever used by clouds ?
the struggle is to keep memory on course
to understand that the day has no reversal
that the other side of time is lost
in the duel between space and light
at its height the sun is an imperfect eye
longing to stay forever at noon
its swart horses its molten chariot
useless in the annihilation of fire
childhood is a black pyramid
whatever follows is a geography
of missing syllables hectares of sound
wheat and gemstones and harvests
weeks that have no location on paper
leaves and their small dark voices
sleeping ever deeper in the Latin
that has been long forgotten

xxxi

we should have listened to the birds !
was it the sun's rifle that got their wings
fractioning the air into multiples of three
branch and leaf hiding places of dew
great axle of the sun turned to pitch and brine !
time to rewrite the famous epics of the sea
heroes of dissolving salt sails flapping wildly
the cigarette of a lifetime and thirst for loves
grown old at the root and sky itself
how did it manage to get lost so fast ?
velvet violet hyacinth mauve fade
arching the brow towards the horizon
and smoke delicate as pearl paste against the wave
talking indolent syllables from time to time
in their sleep the wasted fuming heroes

salt-slap and indigo sheets of air covering
their passage and hoist a derrick troubling
math of the past high toward the wrinkling woof
of clouds a loss of childhood a barely reckoned
poem with its entries of vowel and episodes
circumflex and violent about the sirens
tied to the sleep of others each held to a vow
never to return and the recollection of sand
turning black by noon and the electric fishes
grasping for the light and diving suddenly
into the psyche with its dozens of perforated
pink anemones and smaller still the cries
guttered and wistful of growing old
and cities of grief enormous and distant
alabaster shimmering sugar candy blocks
vanishing as the hour strikes its clock
glassware shattered glittering across
the expanse of purplish waters the waning
and sadness entering the epistles of memory
stepping from summit to summit and highest
the mountain of corrosion and length
separate myths with their hues albescent
and sapphire in the afternoon of grass
when the demons wake from the hunt
and looking more than ever like mortals
pass into a sickness and longing
for days and lives on end this seascape
is all we know 'til our faces
half-eaten by constant spray
turn into the *italics* of an unknown script

this is a mocking bird this a common sparrow
and this the chattering jay
of the dark unnamed wood

xxxii

is firing a shot the definition
that life has more than spent its flame
and plumes diverge and the heart
what of the broken heart ?
and only the white phlox on the silent slope
and because sky is on the edge
of the hill where we lie buried and atop
a cardboard cathedral around which ivy
blackens its savage hours the spires
of living and the toys of breath and light
which women at day's end gather
tired of shadows and envy and talk
of the futility of mountains and seas
the lap lapping of waves against the ear
asleep in the hotel of living to the end
a hand that has lost its shape and
grown dense by twilight and the ivories
of the book and the ruminations of words
that no one has ever heard and the bees
in their swarming alphabet of bright
tired of living as well the wind slackens
near the weeds the stable and the horses
dormant and without luster a dim recall
of the sun whose chariots they used to haul
along paths of fiery elements high above
the sack of routines the opened windows
that look out to nothing and sounds
that deepen in the well where we lie buried
children of the lark the moment of song
in the darkened hillock mourning a loss
eyes alert to the passage and echoes
of gargoyles and saints with tearful eyes
& multitudinous and fateful air
and steles of granite or basalt with

inscriptions of piety and succor for those
diseased from living on earth
and the distant and mountainous languages
of altars and smoking syllables and sacrifices
overwhelming incense broad sheets
lavender and saffron and the grieving
within the knots and vowels
ineffable threnody of oracle and trance
waning memory of grass and its single finger
beckoning night's endless hours
at day's end when women bent over
scour the bottoms for a trace of light
short of breath exhaling
the unheard final word

xxxiii

and Jack lost his wife
just like that a process of syllables
and silences between common words
bread-loaf concentration and granite
speed had nothing to do with it
a lesson in the futility of air
a belief system incapable of holding up
the republic for which it stands
the aerial device extended across
the human brow and perspiration
and muslin or silk what does it matter
the covering of grimace and surprise
archaic vaults with prized stone
gems useless to even let slip
through fingers of envy
a map so intricate only bees
could read it and still go lost
a fable by which to weep with its

multiple tragic endings
outside it was still Saturday
when consciousness could no more
be retrieved and the distant note
of the harp of vanity in the clouds
or the rush of mobile traffic
both profane and divine
in a light aggravated by time's
useless shortcomings
what did Jack know ?
what was not there was
the living breath with its
often florid and poetic contours
the level of darkness spread
immense over the scattered
pinpricks of constellations
in a night without a sky

xxxiv

abyss of mind !
even at high noon the sun's dark empire
holds no light for you
abyss of mind !
angels with hands of surf and fire
circle and circle your intestate chaos
not a song but lamentation of a lifetime
ghosts descend in cryptic elevators
bearing alphabets and palinodes
wandering in a struggle to find grass
by the well's lip where stone bursts in half
a single thought shared by the dead
begins to dissolve at the bottom of salt
cries like waves carried by gulls
back and forth over a tempestuous sea

with nowhere to alight and weep aloud
their intransigent fate
abyss of mind !
know you which of the specters descending
are yours and which belong to the unspoken words
which wounded you in their enormous
passage through a memory riddled by x-rays
and which alone belong to the straits of sound
echoes of echoes ricocheting
through the cliffs and ravines of sleep
abyss of mind !
nothing exists nothing has ever existed
life was a parade of blind statues looking
for a common language
to express the *annihilation* of language
and the denizens of the spirit world
the adolescents now wafer-thin with longing
who have descended to the basement
float as if dazzled by a promise of flame
fireflies and pyramids and stairs
that never reach to the heights
where the outline of a sky wavers
evacuated of all sense and meaning
being slowly erased by moon's fierce insects
abyss of mind !
count no more past three
to embrace the ineluctable phantoms
whose tragic mourning
can never be translated
dense ciphers of the after-world
trapped in the oblivion you created
abyss of mind !

day after day

xxxv

the pharaonic vowel immeasurable as distance itself
buried in the sun's cryptic black stone yearns
for the light of grass for the history of water
revolving around the single finger of clouds
to return to its origins in the empty mouth of time
as we too long to be pronounced in the meridian
before nightfall takes us by the ruins of memory
searching in quiet desperation for our footsteps
for the image of the self on the rock preaching
the vanities and the storms that are our birthright
a frieze of consonants engraved mysteriously
on the parapet of summer that none can decipher
an illusion of the destiny of heat and tragedy alike
the fires lit idly on hilltops that signal an end has come
and flags erected by waves and the shattered masts
the Greeks who have culled our senses in dreams
establishing a fiefdom of sand and cliffs unknown
a Helen who has come and gone in gauze and myrrh
leaving us with some chiffon rags and cheap perfume
evenings in the drill-work of catastrophe and sirens
tickets cut in half for destinations beyond sleep
the pharaonic vowel chiseled hard in the basalt
that extends its arm far into a starless void
can we be other than ourselves our skin and thought ?
or must we remain enigmatic ciphers on the rim
of a great explosion

xxxvi

crucified sun ! black imitation of depths !
fully charged the earth revolves on its own inch
a beast with three personalities and switches
that turn the moon on and off before the storm
seas that surrender only to the small copse

ripe with apples of dissension and statues
that have no middle and turn forever on
the side of emptiness yearning for a language
of smoke and dreams no one can remember or
pronounce because there is a needle fixed in the
sun's opaque heart and there are limitations
to color and time and yet men forge horses
of lead that will fuse to the eye-sockets of Helen !
millennia pass beneath the gravid third of sky
asterisks and insects with the brains of tyrants
immolate the face of history in the famous noun
that ignites by its very sound the passing clouds
above and below the geminated equatorial reflux
oceans of dynamite ! spindled echelons of ink !
everything has been written at least twice now
and the states of the right hemisphere declare war
though there is no trace of the left hemisphere
and the sun's agonized cry to its god resounds
through the pivotal stone and jasmine of creation
geomancy and poetry plot the mercurial city
hundreds of hours pass in a minute and blazes
pour out of fountains and walls start barking
though it is half past noon in the azure plate
the sun is nowhere in sight and heat increases
its diameter and the girls who have pawned
their hair and wrists for ransom drop as if dead
in the plaza and the mechanical ponies go racing
around the diamond spore and it all collapses
day after day going backwards and the jesus
of the apocalypse in tinfoil and glazier's tool
spins in and out like a top denying he is the *same*
the girls ! forgotten by the light's supreme double
sing as never before the plaintive lyric of the islands

crucified sun ! black imitation of depths !

xxxvii

dropped from sight the past an evocation
bucolics and eclogues and smaller repasts
to the ear the slow tide that brings siesta
slumbering in the attic of the bees yellow
swarming in dusty heat and the wound
of life the intransigent thing that won't
go away the vivid remembrances of all
that was sweet and took sick and died
left to wander on the corollary of hills
to the vagabond west of the imagination
slope ravine and desperate arroyo where
sun blasted from its roots crawls to lay
its head on immemorial stone to listen again
for the rivulets of the moon the swooning song
of the ancient stars now a decade past the
limit of memory and oblivion and abed with
memento and charade the overwhelmed mind
with its hands of ritualized consonants that
flutter and shake looking for the archaic
place to rest the slow declining of myth
replete with signs and symbols pointing
always north or east where gods still roam
lost to themselves to their lack of names
to the poetry that excited their existences
the once of a vast and powerful oriental sky
++++++++++++++++++++++++++++++++
we have yet to find the city and its harbor
years and years spent ringing bells and
offering vowels excised from a language
no one has ever spoken and abutting the brow
against the crutch of rock in the highlands
blowsy winds taking bouquets and sprigs
into the air fragrances of the other life
if one could but look back and see as it was

the landscape the beautiful painted drapery
of illusion with its echoing children and
the tiny warfare of thought and longing
instead we cling to these arid final days
searching the clouds for an interpretation
for a meaning to make whole again the light

xxxviii

it has come to this gathered on a spot
just off the sun far away from the concretes
and trees blossoming amidst the blurry traffic
hurrying to work in the oil streams of Manhattan
memory collides with its opposite darkness
lift a winch hoist a sail flap the tarpaulin
shores ferried past their meridian and shouts
gleeful once the trapped insect of mind
now where to go in the roiling waves a transport
of thought a vastness phantom peopled
in shirts and galore of party and alcohol
weave of poetry and sonant gold in the brain
here off the sun a small mercurial outpost
memoried avenues of swift and pointless
direction here and there the grand misinterpretation
stone lions chinked off a cliff and sonnets
or even the epic strut of a movie actor made
to look like the Homeric hero and salt buffs
wafer thin clouds something in the eye
don't cry ! nevertheless the shoulders break
down weeping the solemn moment
when afternoon separates from the main
settled between cocktails a wager to remove
from the hour all vestige of sadness and Egypt
to wake ! the body grown gravid with years
the preponderant missile loses trajectory

Adonis and his fleece of nimble clouds
embanked in a bar on the lower east side
and no Venus to retrieve him from the gutter
you remember how the circus came and
went in tinfoil and grease the plaintive
discord of the organ grinder in his snapped
Italian dialect we all fell down and evening
brought the canvas torn and fluttering over
the trembling firmament of loosened
asterisks and ampersands and what could
we do but stand there stunned agape that life
had such colossal missteps and from the sleeve
of sky issued alternate shadows of hands
nothing to grip but the silhouette in the mirror
the face come undone by nightfall the ear
ringing with the archaic note and sleep

xxxix

the lost galaxies of sleep where the self
is plundered by confusion and the furious asterisks
of identity and loss and the poem itself
is annihilation of the senses a nostalgia
for light a distance equal to blindness
hexameters like waves of the sea rolling out
beyond the hills of transfiguration – a cry !
memory in each leaf in each blade of grass
the intransigent series of masks bidden
and unbidden returned to haunt the sleeper
in a miasma of literature and geomancy
nothing means as it was designed to mean
houses come and go like pools of water
night and the abandonment of time
children wandering in a maze of classes
grammar of the vowel syntax of echo

numbers like birds circling and circling
but never alighting on the parapet of grief
insomnia with its perpetual yellow sandstorms
the Maghreb of longing dotted with minarets
of untranslatable scrolls and muezzins
draped in refinements of cloud and ink
for whom noontimes are an eternity without sky
wheels of voices caravanserais of consonants
detached from the sun of their origins
a red corruption of alphanumeric signs
zodiac of evanescent stellar mansions
evolving from a subliminal peninsula of gas
the shape of mind with its fervent tiny hands
thoughts ideas circles pyramids and commas
galaxies of sleep ! pin pricks in the winds
mountains of chaos where come to rest
the coffin texts of desire and sorrow
accident of life infinitesimal spore
lost in the labyrinths of depth
dust more ancient than space
and space nowhere to be found

xl

no one can count that fast and that far !
and in roman too and beside legions
of sheep curtailed in the dovecote of sleep
who dreams that they have number as well
as fleece and extraordinarily white by dawn
will have been acquitted by some god or other
of his own mortal ignorance for are we not
all as the one who thought light was measurable
and space the equivalent of an afternoon in
some long gone childhood by a riverbank
with trees that margined the road disappearing
into some fairy book of uncut pages and ink

the size of language and metrics and feet
rhyming like leaves in an unblown wind a
sarcophagus too and thoughts like marble
quarried from eternity and putting the head
down on a gravity of rock and listening
for the insistent weeping between lives
how much and how many and yet never enough
always too little and streaming through glass
daylight from another planet a strange chill
as always of an indefinable memory come back
to haunt the shadows in the grass children
most likely who never made it to adolescence
a reverberation inside a tiny bell echoing
for a few instants only before turning dark
the unheard note from a pan's pipe laid to rest
on the other side of the hill where the sun
has gone lost a black stone in endless night
++
the colored thunder in the brain before clock
strikes the uneven hour of spectral collision
to take it all in alphabetizing the grass and
watching the enumeration of dew the weeping
it causes the downright suffering to remember
how each leaf had its portrait stamped on a
paper of wind stained and dissolving lovely
fragrances like the hair of nymphs gathered
on the riverbank to comb the rock of its loss
++
can anything be more beautiful and sadder
than when the universe delicately balanced
on a fingertip explodes in a circus of hues
and echoes and sky unravels a thousand threads
and the child whose hand it was whose fever
it was whose silent voice it was the ineffable
whose last thoughts can never be recorded ?

xli

afternoon concert poems by Eichendorff and Goethe
set to music in the waning light and outside
by the clump of trees eucalyptus and willow
shadow of someone Joe maybe darting in and out
and red how did it get into the poem a distance
or the symbol of longing lost in the tumble of years
what day out of time what hour fugitive and lean
missing from the index and light itself the wan
slanting against a proposal of integers swirling
into the galaxies whose origin is in the Lieder
soprano notes penetrating a geometry of dust
what aches what throbs beneath the heart
an infinite but undefined knowledge that assumes
there are only endings to things memories
curtailed in the vain attempt of the human voice
to meld itself to the sublime as if angels footless
and senselessly tender were just inches away
that we can never be the same again adolescents
who had set out on a journey eons ago amidst
the bric-a-brac of language and higher mathematics
hold out a hand ! what is there if not the impossible
contours of that mysterious red that punctuates
the poem with an Elysium a field of intensity
forever gone the harvests of summers the fields
empire of insects and blind roots groping underneath
perpetual and nostalgic kingdom of Persephone
spreading darkness the conclusion to music

xlii

literal conjectures sun heights described
in hieroglyphs black with ages the dead–time
angels and scorpions each come to the feast
the abandoned table the overturned chairs

despond when zodiac houses start to burn
cold essence of fire the vast empyrean a forest
of blazing vowels stuttering utterances afar
to sleep buried beneath a head of stone and
tumult imagining a summer of lives as brief
as the caterpillar's on its green leaf-meal
consuming the language of air and distance
swept dreams of harvest in the late month
of heat smaller characters type script afloat
in sections of the undiscovered page children
can only read asleep in the dissolved arm
of Morpheus undertaking a voyage to beyond
a symbol in printed grass a fling of thoughts
emptied of content the enormous traveling
of letters through the dizzy transept of mind
look above ! the solar disc as it darkens
hastening the void into a western hill and
to dream of horses made of steam and breath
the suspect gift and to feel if possible the little
that remains of chiseled inscriptions rock
formations hasps and winches of sound
echoing through fingertip and oscillating nerve
to learn then of grief the unexpected day
impossible hour when everything is resolved
in the least detail of smoke and sand and
sorrow lifts its ashen cloak and covers light
so none may recognize the world's shape

xliii

and in what does memory consist if not
of the single blade of grass construed as music
a vanity of winds blowing through the oaten reed
of poetry and excesses of beauty hewn out of
a marble block and *Islands !* the many undiscovered

and floating away from land born mists and
to talk of the day when the most important thing
was the sighting of the god on the ridge just
behind the unbuilt hospital and the arbors delicately
bent as if strewn out of a declining moon at pre-dawn
wave-lengths of echo and leaves whispering names
forbidden and enigmatic meant to reach the ear
of stone and there remain buried and untranslated
and the *Book of the Dead* memory's finest monument
invisible and ineffable with its galactic extensions
pyramids of yellow pollen and histories of bees
interwoven with a theogony composed of sand
and the unspeakable pharaonic Eye in the middle
of the *res gestae* wherein are accounted the origins
of honey the value of mountains and the wars
between statue and myth and always the talking
in sleep the wandering plague of thoughts at noon
the rush of oriental seas to take the emperor's knees
how do such afternoons come to pass ? laying the head
on the rock abutment to listen to the years as
they pass through defiles in Anatolia yet how little
has changed since the invention of the wheel
and the astrolabe and the location of the Sun !
blackness is the where of memory blank evaporations
tiny footnotes written in steam at the end of life
and to look for memory on destroyed lawns
not far from the road that led half way up to the sky
traces of dew where memory went extinct
a child's voice murmuring deep within the vowel
that floats forever into the vast Unknown

xliv

poetry they say can only go so far
the summer rock the dashing stream

shadows interlaced with eternal silence
voices that perhaps never were but drugged
ornaments of sound and distance irretrievable
an afternoon just once between what is learned
and what is just as soon forgotten like echoes
rills and silvery curlicues of water rampant
in the sylvan conjunction that separates
life from death can only go so far
up a woven stair of smoke and magic signs
flashing on and off with a purplish thunder
clouds and denials of reason and tender
blossoms that fade no sooner touched
pale crescents in the violet evening dun
hills that evaporate and turn to ether longing
that comes undone when the first star rises
out of its poignant mathematics in an oriental myth
can only go so far poetry they say a madness
interjected in the transient brain a lamp
shedding peculiar luster over the darkened hour
a foreboding in the ear of stone a sand bank
crumbling in night's dense passage
the no more of *this* the even less of *that*
vowels intaglios of once bright effulgence
when memory loses all contour and definition
AOI the hand and its leaf !

xlv

how many to count the dead and not just the dead
but the many deaths of each of the dead and to recall
the color green even the sun was green that day
the dead in their circle of daisies and daffodils
the urgency to know how it happened when nothing
at all happened but turned to stone and to blackness
the knife cutting the air into hemispheres of cruelty

and delusion the multiple dead really only the one
that mattered on his single straw with his palm and
strewn to the side the remains of what he last saw
a shard a broken pitcher a part of a painting in red
and darkness surrounding the smallest part of a
hill receding from the center and what a barking
a dog long dead now its tail curled and evening
setting in its glassy eyes and green the sun ever greener
but losing its warmth and going down into the stone
deep into the stone the eventuality of a fan colored
faint Chinese tones or silk and arabesques wrapped
around the face of the dead the many still to be
numbered on one hand the thumb like an iris on canvas
and the dusty something of memory even this afternoon
the vivid the quick the sharp outline on the other side
of a world made of glass and the rotundas of fire
centuries old now or just the deaths of the minute
gathered into an anthology withered petals faded hues
this afternoon's realization the poems forming a rush
like underground water striking the impediment and
Etruscan versions of Persephone and her mate the king
of the underworld and knee to the softness and shoulder
yoked to an invisible light and thrusting forward
like a moon of the dead the rug just lying there a
mottled green a lasting fuse of distance a made-up
past fiction of awnings and a traffic of mules carrying
bodies to the common ground smell of automotive oil
in the air the stifling atmosphere of the dead who are
keeping something inside them a secret we cannot ever
know the afterwards of a tomorrow crystallized like sugar
but forgotten too the very shape of time the dime or
angry penny lying on the counter stiff hands supposed
to conjecture a wealth the fantastic black hoard of the
dead

xlvi

And in my minde I measure pace by pace
To seke the place where I my self had lost
              Henry Howard, Earl of Surrey

where trees are taught to memorize the griefs
and sorrows of mortals who pace in their shadows
lamenting the birth of time the source of light
that ever woe to each was born and the longing
for distances unkenned the marvel of memory
that mind holds captive in its dissonance
and the tangle of silk and russet cloths in sleep
and fever's unrequited dreams of a sea too vast
to cross unless in a coffin floating ever east
where mountains in their size still lack capacity
to sympathize and dwindle valleys in the purple
of descending night and errant spirits from leaf
to leaf dialogue with one another though to each
the face remains unrecognized through branches
which a rare breeze unwinds and prepares for
torment and skies capsized and thunder's blooms
iridescent in the vacant gloom and loud the war
between vowel and sybilline descant a ringing
that music derives from the dance of shades
Orpheus on his rock Linus buried in his string
what intestine syllables what ravaged wound
that never runs dry the life of man the smallest
day in its volume of pressed flowers and decay
and to stars blame the fates and turning from
the self the self denies this enigmatic plight
so precious that remote and ignorant summer
when what was to be had already come to pass

xlvii

with my brother we float across random lawns of sky
serenities of buffered cloud cliffs of woven honey
patterns of an archaic and broken language that vie
for memory in our common shadow and mind
across multilayered histories of a single kingdom
that a man could in a simple day traverse ourselves
a flute and bone and text of interwoven grasses worn
like sleeves of wind and words that in a rush manifest
and sound like distant echoes in our rampant ear
to each the other turned a face of summer longing
remembrance of places only we could have ever known
stoned pyramids drugged plazas of an ivy-girt tropic
metals and moons and brilliant vowels that fluttered
like hair in the nocturnal syllable of time each the other
the non-plussed and ragged shirt meant to be shared
upon waking in this newfound crescent of life above
ever dizzying heights of noun and sublime adjective
an afternoon forever ! spoken like a blade of grass
between us in this vast wandering hive of poetry
yet wounds and engines and violent accents above
a shattered complex of understanding and confusion
as to which shoulder fits the barrow and which knee
goes first in the forward agony of separations
hands that articulate the course of eternal return
crystal corners ricocheted glass that has no reverse
mutilations of the drugstore clock and metamorphosis
of the only book there is in the children's reading room
length of autumn curtains and sadness in the sunset leaf
hills where sorrow is quarried for its Aztec breadth
and always the always that never comes to be as
we float on random lawns above turquoise heavens
byzantine reliquaries shivers of deranged conquistadores
infants in the puzzling maze of great Chapultepec
to learn to sleep alone ! rooms and runes and shards

of the complete unknown and avenues on maps
we drew to assure space of its insignificance
now withered specters in oblivion's Etruscan fane
how soon before I how soon before I with Joe return ?

xlviii

> *"Dov'erano gli scarafaggi dell'ultima estate, le formiche, I ragni? Passano le stagioni, come passano!"*
>
> *Fausta Cialente, Cortile a Cleopatra*

the last of the moon in recorded time
appeared like a silver object on the painted fans
of her eyelids it was mysterious enough that world
governance was turned over to insects and mists
nay swarms of winged things gnats bees flying bugs
enough of the nightmare the recourse was to
an alternative to reason and reality to skies underscored
by nebulous lesions to the abandoned quarters
of the gods now only slimy snail traces on the floor
of the running motor and despite the overwhelming
grief was in order the statues of reply and demand
the talking still in the learning stages and interpretation
of the signs digital references to memory whose
recording was now nothing but an interrupted series
of light playing in the frail windswept hair of children
names but not substance in the recall of the months
sorrowing floral patterns faded in the winch of the hills
slowly moving toward their seedbed in the west
of the orient and how loud the command from clouds
the insistence to redesign the cities of the lake
immolated faces appearing momentarily on
the watery surface of sleep and the peculiar monument
erected overnight on the front lawn where fireflies
worship the aging cosmos a matter of sand and wattle

doorways of perception the porches where dancers
perfect their silhouettes and ink drapes its cypresses
with an inchoate oblivion that we cannot return
and stone fused to the planet Nemesis and what
is it deep within the heart that shifts red
with a pre-historic cunning the aggravated airs
the volcanic miasma the unwritten poetry used as
barter among the chthonic deities who still keep house
below the marshes of human consciousness if only
the seasons did not pass so swiftly last summer's
cockroaches ants and spiders where have they gone ?

xlix

a short poem about the showers sweet their death
in May the lovers' wont and clouds excel on pointed
reefs and heavens where no boneless god relieves
uneven number and spaceless boundaries the end
of all short poems the brief and weeping disconsolate
when recalling moments all too short the rains
that compelled the eye to turn and sleep that gave
the poem its brief and dreams of countless animals
of blind and young the thing working in the grass
the leafy shoots the sprouts and buds that lovers
embrace in their deluded guise and high above the
cloudless element the poem with its clay and subtlety
the legends spun the strings undone the colors bright
the hue and echo in each untrammeled verse a traffic
of fireflies and midges the nodding assent of death
the palace underneath the worms' abode that yawns
like an abyss for all the poem curtailed in its sweet
recall and endless rhymes in the mouths of bards
whose dying breath is legend in the leaf and green
as ever the new-born sun turning darker as noon
is won and grief the upper hand maintains while

light seeks refuge in the bane and all but hills
in shadowy disdain keep moving slowly to the end
this little poem about springtime's alert these words
fashioned from the sorrowing pen and the brain
itself in its sink and pan can but weep the memory
of one clad in the cloth of merciless childhood so
brief as is this poem for no one sung but loss

1

we are in the latitudes of time where each hour
drips its continent and shades of large wailing
the shores dispel with a commerce of frugal light
small remembrances of the other life before space
began the hills and treetops the bunting and sparrow
the song-life of minds unborn the relay of error
unto each breath a life to come a day a rushing
at the ankles of grass in burrows and coves asleep
who will recount the narrative of the *day before*
the single rain drops the eclipse in the eye of moon
and splendors unrevealed in syllables of long descant
the endless stone sunk in the sun's middle track
where struggles green with wraiths of watery air
and nymphs at once on rocks that sing their hair
wash in everlasting vowels like hail and thunders
and longing like an ivy trumpet their being fills
to see at every turn love's emblem burning seal
that closes noon before it starts and fires colder
than the untilled soil of night oh that other dawns
and eon of leaf and talking verdigris and marble
that stands on stilts of poetry and from deep within
the heart's oldest core the silvery zone of dreams
spent ere the lid reveals the newer day of time where
we still walk unknown phantoms endowed with speech
traversing libraries of foil and tenderness and reach

higher than above our hands grope to obtain again
their shape the yearning summers the rills and wells
where faces dip looking for their masks and reflecting
pools of thought that confuse the overture of unheard
notes the grace of voices sublime and lost the ear
spent in musk the depths of green and mossy reveries
children released from boundaries left to mingle
in the small heat of envelopes with buried names
freight of airless memory the end of time's refrain

li

now comes time of Kaliyug short life span greed
intoxication and gambling in excess palaces losses
selfish gains and forgetfulness the end of honor
and honesty thugs and forgers and politicians
reign of sulfur and opium cities sunk in mud flats
waters malevolent and poisoned on the rise about
to drown book by book memory of recorded history
Kaliyug of the yellowing grasses of misspent fingers
of numerals cast in blood spinal artifacts and x-rays
deceptions of interior design lunations and trances
walls shifting of their own accord towards a mythology
of lies lexicons of deceit price warfare over condolences
funerary steles erected at noon dishonoring recent
warriors now outfitted in rest homes of decrepitude
orange hair and violent repetitions of a single vowel
what's to salvage ? wrathful Nemesis heading for
planet earth foaming surges of atomic tidal waves
can one hand save the other ? love and devotion
draped in blue antinomy desires rapture of godhood
falsified illegible texts hornets jackals and hoot-owls
Kaliyug Kaliyug Kaliyug time to grieve and mourn
hours of bad rain of uranium clockwork and clouds
of splintered bone in the eye's forlorn text reading

backwards through the dead puranas lifeless copper
formless zinc abyss of bedtime stories unparalleled
cells dormers for serpent and demon and phantom
spirits that cannot be liberated from the body issues
and advertisements for the end of time and ghouls
draped like ivy around the goddess of insomnia
white wraiths ! fields yoked to cross-eyed oxen
hills filled with unpaired nails love and devotion
starved in the prison house of knowledge et cetera
Kaliyug is yesterday Kaliyug is tomorrow is no day
at all is in the newspapers and magazines and dentist
offices and on the sidewalk with the homeless selling
hoodoo dust and vermin and headless worms that
till the underground and by three in the afternoon
when dark is at its highest power and howling and
lamenting fill the ambulances and sorrow evermore
and fire is stricken from the core throats turn blue
and shaking in the pulse the mountain lays down
its weary stone epitome and all light is lost
Kaliyug ! the small red thread that zigzags through
the bottom of sand the slightest fist and verse
love and devotion in the conch shell's echo and
in the minute rattle of silver anklets and finally
in the remotest corner of the universe where
space and time have nowhere else to go
Kaliyug !

lii

heaven in a fist full of worm meal
cyanide and blossoming hyacinth
the labors of light to bring forth breath
a rendering of clouds nil abstract floating
a sleep without purpose dived deep
into the inky chasm recollection of hands

skin and mind and the thin carapace of thought
was this the element ? using ampersand
and vowel loosened from the cataract
of sound the verse begins in its middle
wave upon wave of undefined waters
the shoreline itself the last thing seen
before going under in a torment of syllables
rounding the cape and the helmsman drunk
with vision of the starry void above
and how it all comes together just once
a design taken from the blackboard where
conjugated verbs seem to take flight
from their chalky afternoon exercise
and into the deep gloaming the chaotic
tangle of consonant and question mark
the raveling of metaphor and simile and
celestial interjections as if to inform the *Poem*
of its essence its swarming luster quivering
just inches from the surface of sky
and being written and erased and
brought to the margins and employed
a lexicon of archaic stone of grass and seed
and number which is rhythm and meter
and aloft the crazy directionless words
a goddess describe her dazzling raiment
stepping as she does from rock to rill
and the suspense of her eyes darting
to the branch where the hive hangs
a thing waiting for night the infused
and inspired dream talking as statues
in the noon of their creation blazing
alabaster and marble and the final
epoch of dust when history has been
forgotten and clambering over temple ruins
goat and satyr stir the air for a volume

of enigma opening vast pages of formulae
mysterious as the rhetoric of leaves
in the puzzling literature of memory

liii

sun blossoms imported from the continent of light
valleys deep and capacious and hills where mysteries
evolve their vowels so much like distant glass and sorrows
woven between the vast conjunctions of time and
the ever circling sky with its layers of ether and flame
so much that cannot be comprehended the slender
moons that slide through the crevices of night slowly
opening their argent wounds and disappearing
amongst the myriad alphabets of the galaxies
and grief and the patient leaves that shake aloud
in the hive's somnolent ear and the language of statues
and the quarries that lie beneath the seas of memory
how much light has given and for us to breathe
in its only summer phantomatic conjectures of
person and soul and the give-and-take of masks
the tiny accidents of writing that number the grass
a fiction of seasons in the warehouse of dreams
the impotence of still another hour turning on the wheel
how many bodhisattvas how many bodies that come
into being and pass away into the enormous silence
what are the things that lean against the wall and cry
where will it go when it is put out at last the light ?
shadows of mind uncertainties imperfections *thought*
the error of ascribing eternity to the missing finger
of going round and round in the pit where a city was
and erecting stone effigies and pouring libations
to the already dead and the boats hauled from sleep
and the sands that travel with the figures of youth
girls like fireflies dancing with silhouettes on the porch

and the lads in their gravel and ropes and pools learning
to die when the water fills its inch and the clouds
go rushing through the green infinity of echo BANG !
we are each in the uncounted graph of the missing and
disappeared tongues and syllables and lapses of sound
bewilderment of waking on a planet secretly burning
the phases of a lamp slopes and flickering distances
sun blossoms lowering their brief heads and hands
from nowhere come to pluck their anthology
a darkness of pre-history and stone a mythology
the ineffable sequences of a long unremembered past

liv

news in from the other side of the hill
false medical reports sun slants in wrong direction
a history of grass for middle school readers
the alphabetarian of death with his knuckles
and spools and tinfoil shields a prediction
of war in the Gulf and radio relays of voices
long gone at the whistle-stop
is memory only decay ? is there a full stop ?
the remains of the uncounted and their polygraph
long nights of dream-siege of sand and rope
where are they coming from the depths
with their intonations of guilt and denial
after all these decades and only the darkening
the missing corners the steps that fail going down
wired misconnections to a Homeric abyss
going round and round the specters pleading
for a glass of light for a comb for a shoe-lace
abandoned as we all are in the last act
this is age of forgetting and confusion
names and the sticker tags that go with them
does the doorbell buzzer still work ?

which is the way to the kitchen and which
the exit to hell cobwebs and scrapers
linoleum cuts don't fit feet otherwise missing
verses every morning about ideal landscape
noble shepherds love sick at the heart and lost
in their visualized hexameter of mountains
for all the world it seems *real* and the languages
that match with inflexion and code and accent
perpetuating a myth about the past
peninsula and rock and godhead of voyages
to found realms that will last forever !
still there is the motor to worry about
the blood-sugar and hemoglobin count and
the prescriptions that have been recalled
how does one keep up with the months ?
soon it will be *never* and longing and sorrow
at the bedpost tied like an unwilling ghost
what life was sleeping in the deadened nerve
an afternoon with balloons and bubbly soda
zapped by a switch
lights out

lv

where silence and darkness intersect
and what lies beyond that point night
emerging from the taint of space
an idea alone like gravity moving
clouds across fields of summer grass
sudden as childhood's loss in an instant
to recall which day it was which hour
surrounded the accident to invoke
the myth of red dissolving in a fever
gone circling an unseen planet within
the terminus of possibility and grief

and striking glass as if to evolve words
from a dissemination of accent and
vowel leaves begin their dark speech
revolving memories recitations of water
depths intransigence and brooding
that cannot be reached and great sleep
shapeless and infinite in its minute
boundaries if that is what happens
in the parenthesis of breath and light
a suffix of air attached to the noun
meaning sky and troubling flashes
ancient as rock and gathered gravel
in the small pit where knee grazes
immemorial distance falling from its
own discourse of parts into a cavity
of lunar dimensions whitening thought
as it unravels in a pool without surface
to speak of the ends of things nightly
taking turns with the other to forget
what was learned daily over and over
hand defies shape and mind's shadow
goes walking alone into the gloaming
guided no more by the stellar paths

lvi

to the southernmost isle the abode of the dead
keeping in mind the oncoming rains the winds
the seeding and the new leafage and how green
must the horizon be for the dead in their floating
island a mansion a hotel a room with proper parts
and the wailing and remembering and flickering
candles can barely see two ells in front and to be sure
is that Joe on the extreme left and the ghostly sigh
a whisper betraying bodily torments exiguous

as the voice lost in the desert sands the smallest
the frailest recognition like a photograph blown up
and suddenly sent into remission to reappear
six decades later of Joe and his half leaning against
the invisible world a parapet of tumbling summers
vain automobile excursions to Hades and back
thick dense rope of water underneath no reflections
only miasma and dereliction and the contours
of the several months it takes to ripen death's holiday
a riot of song and immersion and nocturnal flight
the stars ! verdant clusters of bright and shining
like burgeoning grapes held high in Bacchus' fist
everything is unseen and time is no greater than
the thumbnail of a friend disappearing in the dark
can their faces be so handsome so doomed to ruin ?
in the ear the running and rushing of the years
no sense can be made of the metal where sleep
is manufactured nor of the boundaries of space
infinitesimal grass weaving through fingers
abstractions called art and history and enormous
conflagrations on the other side of the sun
blackening just as Joe is turning to soot and ash
except for the face captured by light and for a moment
only as vivid as still-life allows far from the truth
to the southernmost isle the abode of the dead
long nights together sewn within the lunar dream
wet peril of the Pleiades and house of Aquarius
and Zeus standing great in girt and height
shaking prepared to hurl his missile

will Augustus be pleased with this poem ?

lvii
(for Laurita)

mother issuing from the realm of the dead
stands shaking ever so slightly on an illusory porch
something in her hands must be the shape of distance
and what is she trying to articulate what can be
pronounced from the remote incision of time
where she appears wavering pale deformed leaf
torn from a willow branch in some lost summer
do the dead shed tears do they dry their eyes
can they see beyond time present into the past
of the future in a confusion of verbal tenses
she seems to be gesturing pointing to *somewhere*
there are low lying bushes an arroyo a purring
rumble of diesel engines forging a highway east
memory of rust of dew hanging in the early sheen
names that do not consolidate into syllables
vatic utterances is that what she is attempting
like a Sybil trapped in glass her eyes betoken
warnings deaths to come months unraveling
like desiccated tobacco leaves ocher brown
an atlas unearthed by her feet gnarled smoke
patterns indicating sunken harbors cities of pearl
magnets that hold the sky in place red shifts
in the heavens of sleep the marginless defiance
of space truncated by her eerie manifestation and
heat turning into corollaries of afternoons on hills
just to the south and west of her puzzling etymology
mother ! one of us never sure which shouts
an anvil drops from nowhere a horse whinnies
verses recited from the depths of an Etruscan tomb
or the sound of a lawn mower tunneling a siesta
out of the dense tropical air for if nothing else
she is an advertisement for humidity a drenched paper

a translation of pyramid speech into levers of sand
her biblical remonstrance orders a black sun
to remain purulent in the opaque summer firmament
soon she will disappear like an opalescent evening
tired of trying to be heard and saddened by all
that has happened since she last appeared in
the sanitarium oracular as a homophone of light
gesticulating wildly pointing at *something*
the music she was before we were born and
the dance of gauze and veils and an old radio
echoes of winters darkening by three PM
when identities dissolve and stories stay untold
the last of her is a wisp of hair once auburn
the enormous invisibility of the cosmos is all now
an inarticulate snowfall that obliterates memory
lawns and streets and terraces with swings going
to and fro in the attic where we try to sleep
anxious for mother to come home again

lviii

stood for what seemed like hours in front of
the library a day a month fifty minutes the sun
rained down on us puzzling over the liquid fragments
of the oracle we were to decipher for the exam
and for the duration asked ourselves whether
we were to pass from this planet without having seen
the antiquities of Sicily the great temple ruins
of Segesta or Taormina and to be in awe of Aetna
in rolling hexameters and looking at one another
elements of American history bogs and marshes
the wars of 1812 or 1898 what of them the doors
brassy and carved with intricate figures both classical
and biblical and waiting there was it the photographer
who would render us futile and eternal the girls

coming from behind in pinafore and pearls
they held the secret to the mystery of virtually
everything the passing seasons the steps that go up
but not down and the first cigarette with its
intoxicating bluish smoke becoming one with
the heavens standing there book and compass in hand
the voice of the Sybil issued with an unexpected ring
asking us whether we wanted to die and the sound
of afternoon motor traffic and the stillness in each
leaf and the hymns of birds before daybreak
the world had never seemed so imminent and distant
in the next instant grown to the likeness of manhood
some of us disappeared or perhaps dead already
who of us knew the other ? hands a-tremble the hair
oiled and parted on the head and the sacrifice
which is knowledge and the words of the Sybil
how far south they were how out of reach still ringing
and then the carillon struck five PM and a hush
an enormous dread spread throughout the city
windows came and went reflecting nothing and
we began to scatter going different routes towards
homes that had become strange and evenings
issuing from the western hills and the chill of the air
still the words of the Sybil enigmatic and potent
stirring in our ears as we fell into a sleep of stone
and the grass which was a dream and the oracle
string of senseless syllables sounding in the night
as far as the stars now green with memory
and soon to fade

lix

works of art of the imagination great works
established for all time as masterpieces when
shepherds cloaked as civilization and walked

in umbratile groves spreading discourse to
memorize other fragments like stone effigies
learning to speak as if it were possible for marble
quarried from islands of the imagination great
islands masterworks for all time with cypresses
that touch heaven and fabric and silk and gold
interwoven in the fine stuff and images drawn
and sewn and creations of the mind vast and
speaking to the heart the deep rivers the subtle
hierarchies of idea and touch and still the hand
looking for its shape and sleeping repose leaf
upon leaf dreaming darkest the interior of
man's finest like silhouettes of ink stretched
against the sky wings beating faint at first
then louder in the ear a music to wonder at
great compositions for timbrel and rebec and
shapes of notes ascending seraphic beams aimed
at the most of memory the part that has shorelines
an abundance of rock and high resounding surf
waves that take up the history of time and such
a brief respite when the body needs must lie down
and seek shelter from the scourges the illumined
manuscripts the borderline figments and fictions
a person has to read these things and report
afterwards and ascribe to others what is his own
how can it be these odes epics Levantine scripts
these in fact biblical tomes and prophesies are
to be mastered in a day and lie the head down
in its own abyss trying to recall in desperation
the first few lines the invocations to the Muse
the lives of heroes too short lived the end of things
in a blast of sand and high octane flame moon
and sun and pyramid and understanding nothing
of what has happened living a twilight life sad
wondering what is the size of light or where

night goes when the hills disappear and writing
over and over the same word in a thousand
tongues language itself an appendix to breath
a threat to organization eking out from shelves
of discarded libraries evolutionary drifts of mind
the orient capsized in a birthright and mendicants
door to door begging for just a page a single page
of all that has been jotted down considered too late
for the afternoon and put to bed and given waste
to dream apart from the planet's collision course
hermeneutics and translations and always error
misunderstanding of what was meant and intended
in the great works of art the imagination frayed
consequences of interpretation a mountain or cliff
scribbled like calligraphy on the horizon setting
lamps dotted acres of stubble leftover suffixes
to a lexicon of pre-historic poetry unwritten
and devoured by miasma and sand reddening
in the galactic scripture of midnight a billion
asterisks going *ping!*

lx

and in this day in time—what is it ? a Monday
they were plotting to send you off from the rafters
a glee in their brazen spirit copper reflections of breath
mitigated by the window's somnolent refraction
like a suspended water and kept the machines going
constant hum and dring and oscillating needles
between the various but imagined nation states
however much disbelief was in the atmosphere
rumpled bed clothes inconstancy of the nurses
in their sidelong glances an arm here a leg there
reinforcements always too late for the soul already
planning to levitate before three days were up

all efforts to conceal the truth wrapped clumsily in
yellowed sheets the mess in the middle being the body
the wayward thing tossed all these years from sea
to sea in tempest and wind gales and wailing noise
of waves out of control to reach the burdened skies
cliffs dimly perceived in distances of routine medical
rounds the flinty spell of scientific lore words invented
to disguise the human condition in all its errant
splendor and grief the little notches the frayed inches
skin itself the song of fever and illusion belonging
and not belonging names and egos and frustrations
of myth—will it happen today and how and if?
the always interpolated sighs the conjectures as to
time and its grafted planets of misspent hours going
but not returning through corridors lacking exits
rattle of a rickety elevator wheezing through floors
of existence and the lurching halt of *being* somewhere
between an unmarked door and the broken levers
how will tomorrow differ from today in the swirling ballet
of promises and prevarications set in porous rock
to lay the head down finally beyond the whine of sirens
in the vast potential of ether outside the source of rain
darkness in the sudden side-street and perpetual twilight
at the bottom of the unnamed mountain just waiting
in that small space where wheels can no longer turn
how little was the specter of joy its flickering lamps
one by one the harp notes ascend into silence
the multiplied Mondays become smoke

the multiplied Mondays become smoke

lxi

Felix, qui potuit rerum cognoscere causas
atque metus omnis inexorabile fatum
subiecit pedibus strepitumque Acherontis avari.
          Virgil, Georgicon liber II, 490-492

on the rim of time where everything is identical
on one side or the other the sensation is the same
the burn the cut the beauty perceived and felt
to the bone a symphony orchestra of equal parts
string drum and horn sharing the same note
ascending into some seraphic otherness of being
where the pathologies of identity no longer matter
you and I everything we heard was simultaneous
we were both vice versa in front of the big electric
music box our hemispheres already confused and
wired to each other so front was back and side-
ways was left handed a hairline parting the two
continents of the other uncounted hemisphere
so big and wide and large we were asleep inside
each other in front of the big electric juke box
fused to an orient of dissolved lunations humming
like swarms of mythical bees mountains capsized
in the thimble we shared whenever daylight broke
the record of its own eternity and which was how
and why we were easily mistaken for the small letters
that begin with aleph and end in rust unequivocal
members of the selfsame motor running long enough
for sleep to switch its inks turning circles backwards
through galaxies known only to pyramid-walkers
for us the black sun cremated a summer of poetry
season of cities incised in a block of parian marble
deft as grasshoppers or fireflies we played in grasses
that grew five miles high in a trance of archaic stone
history played its bongos zithers and Aeolian harps

between captivity and isolation and ivy-girt Memory
bade each of us to be fac-similes of *someone else* in time
unrecognized phantom child lost in a winter maze
oracular raving of the heart's lone vatic soul
how many thousands of crepuscules ago that was
the month of ninety nine moons the talking *leaf*!
lifelong ambition to return one to the other and
forever forget a ten minute hiatus separates us
to this day on time's infinite and invisible rim
you on the dead side I still breathing on the other

lxii

suncloud burst ! purple months ! stratigraphies of mind !
you said it--colloidal seas and numinous geologies of air !
in a spin the metabolism of myth and arithmetic and
what do we get ? loss and longing and oblivion
forgeries of memory grasses implanted on the backside
of a wayward thought about the gods how long will they be
where will they stay this winter what is hapax legomenon ?
lunar topographies of the soul and bands of angels
blinding white fusions of salt and alabaster ascending
weightless and footless the deviant alien spirit free !
children come and go in the span of flashlight batteries !
corollaries of summer in a single dewdrop malingering
on the tip of a syllable turning green and weaving
reflections of speech patterns glossed in the wan light
of a month that lacks beginning and end a counterfeit !
it goes on and on the decibels of sleep crashing
in an ear of water somnolent specters raise their glasses
high into a borrowed season of heat and iridescence
luminous ciphers with zodiacal names and fire storms !
the petty humble and small voices that plead inside the leaf
what must be ! in a single day empires of insects blow !
fingers of missing alphabets and crowns of vowels blazing

in the museum of art-history ! has not everything been
accounted for in the cumulative index of absence and reason ?
to a man are allotted but a smattering of dialects
illustrations of time on the margins tiny red dots
squiggles and ampersands and decades no more than ten
each hand is a bastion of numerology blind gropings
into the theory of death before birth and the sorrowing
and grief implicit in each consonant in the hierarchies
of sand and wind—leave the Pharaohs their eyes of dust !
to hazard a guess as to what follows the knee on its altar
or how long shoulders can bear mortal fragility
it is time for the accent to receive its final direction
over which hieroglyph must it be placed and in what order ?
leave well enough alone to the afternoon of ceremonies !
ink blotters and tables moving mysteriously commanded
by the dead and shipwrecks in the bed chamber !
grammar ! mummers of chalk ! eight times eight !
to sleep again despite the errors of punctuation slots
where undeliverable mail goes and weeping profusely
a man is only so much a tear-duct a trembling lip
a siphon into which are poured the lees of biography
and nothing more

lxiii

(a)

what ends in the photograph is time
light captured ravished by shadows
masks that in space freeze their features
no sound alerts the chorus of winds
no green sprouts intrude their lusty growth
a footfall is all the song one can surmise
and brother and his peers all sweet
their hair a lyric upswept and languished
here come the undertakers in their leaf

and the verbiage of air and passing cloud
the riot of memory when the silent sea
took the shore with waves raining photons
what is the other side of light if not the moon
with its marks of beautiful irregularity ?
poem of the sun blackening in the heart
and planets invisible and unnamed that
steam coursing through eyes held fast
their aim the unseen god who directs
with unerring dart their swift demise
outside the frame beyond the camera's pulse
the lens stained with keen foreboding
a day will come when fading all will fail
the bright of that summer hour the dense
shape of the unknown moving like a knife
through discourse and reason and smiles
and brittle celluloid reversed and smaller
still the imperceptible inch of reverie
the catch in the throat the illusory index
when no number exists to realize time
in the chiaroscuro mausoleum of loss

(b)

hibiscus and rhododendron steep climbing
the light's false cliff you who was but one
among the trembling blooms your face a fuse
charged against diminishing time the high
and illusive idea of image impressed
like a thumb of ink upon vanishing air
a page or two scramble of sybilline sounds
interpretations of wind beating in the void
and sky's ever azure assumptions making
of *that* day the only one a leaf perfected
in its hue by the mind's undressed rhetoric
a vast a tomb a style a phrase broken

into figures multiple by two and dense
the grass dry in its bent hemisphere a lure
to flame and weed alike the rounded cavity
where thoughts go buried in miasma dark
to hold the pose and strike the brow with ice
like glass shatters all around the atmosphere
a holy once then fall down shoulder knee
and shadow convicted in the camera's eye

lxiv
"words lost their significance"
E. Pound

mysteries of the afternoon promenade
through glass and trance the sky a refulgent
oriental saffron seen through the eyes of one
long gone and the hedges where they hide
the siege works and the elopements from
last night's dream promising with all your heart
words don't matter she bristles can barely
recognize who she is and the shifts in time
the parallel lives and the ones that don't count
anymore and words what are they seed bed
of misunderstanding and broken promises
wake up and writhe fall back asleep number
the ink on the sprawling wall of space and
try to figure which star is yours up above
your fickle faithless head the knots untie
history has no order to it a fractured
sequence of lacunae and alphabets gone
awry and words what can they mean when
void and vacuum and emptiness are all about
the game plan is crumpled plot of roses
and insects have the day buzzing and sawing
through matter into a fourth dimension

awnings sprawl like clouds dense and dark
the chill is there at a loss for words you
circle back looking for the library door
steps and smoke and windows boarded up
names as well and flights of fancy in ocher
and dotted Tuscan umber illustrated pages
turning in the brisk autumn wind of memory
paragraphs of deleted thoughts mind itself
at sea in a quandary as to language and
divinity the darker *Muses* that wrangle
human motives and make of beauty
a wordless splendor cosmic and irrelevant

lxv

gathered the gods together as a unit and
troubled of mind and confused as to action
to the milk-sea descended to consult *Narayan*
gift holder doctor of internal medicine from
whom all narrates and the *two* dissolves
into the *one* and heads bowed hands folded
assuming the lotus seat praying with both knees
murmuring centuries' old vedic ritual mumbo
thumb to lip hair shorn only a top-knot left
eyes turned inside out the cosmos began to
revolve within the brain's tiny visual apparatus
star-flung punctuations cattle floods mountain
torments sexual indispositions male becoming
female the juggernaut rolling its wheel of
purpose over the earthly detritus and flotsam
for a savior to manifest ! Indra Rudra Shiva Vishnu !
four-faced Brahma become an aggregate of
intricate rock sculptures hanging in midair
what hand can ever unravel the mysterious
and incoherent vowels the syllabary of phonetic

dissolution the babble and mechanics of language ?
finger topples graveyard elephant ruts on brow
dream-stuff cycles rutilate inside the mind's
illegible topography drainage system and sand pile
wharfs where the dead stagger looking for a thimble
massive accident of human history and laws !
writing from right to left and down to up
the great symbolisms of discourse and madness
the Eye ! five-fold galaxies spinning out of control
on the colossal fingertip of Devotion //
and how many times and how often has
everything happened over and over and skies
and the skies that exist behind the skies roaring
infinitely in the enormous stone ear of the Buddha
insect music ! cadavers of fire ! the end !
eschatology of the Infinite sewn in ether
and I who have become the honorific Pronoun
who ramble and wander and totter on the brink
of endless sleep and you wherever have you gone ?
there is no other *other* !

lxvi

goddess , the , of vowels totally constructed
infinite as air space or ether the light she devours
to feed the poets who aimlessly assemble consonants
obstructions of pure sound the valleys and depths
below the reverberating flame which is her mind
fleet in principle winged of foot wavering shimmer
in the bright holograph of noon to the east and south
before the birth of language out of rock and grammar
of stolen love to be memorized as are the grasses
grown over night on the slope facing boundless water
goddess , the , sonic depths unhindered by letters
roaring in the ear's small chasm where sleep informs

the poets who learn in vain words of chalk and ink
I am the was of where the ancient stone and number
clicks and glottal stops and retroflex dentals surds
the empire of syntax forever dissolving aphonic
as the mountain whence spring the muses
swift as the utterances of the goddess whom
they represent in the immense flurry of wind and sea
tempests of brain and shattered thumbs
sails and riggings of *memory's* lost summer
stammering over and over the entranced poet
sitting on his porous meter ivy-twined staff in one hand
the other revolving a small crystal globe the *world* !
goddess , the , ever elusive her magic of vowel and spark
blazing peacock and brazen faced monkey cavort
in her passage and whole epics a hundred books long
come and go through the dense jungle of verbiage
a single minute carved out of the unfinished hour
sages and heroes and violent women and trees
no place for the foot ! at arm's length the silhouette
always bright and illusory shedding vowels to the winds
goddess , the , a brace of scattering deer spotted
and wild eyed recalling their human pre-birth
dash across the Deccan in a matter of centuries
earth of lush liana great elephants erupt from cliffs
bruiting loud and enormous the red of dawn
as it comes down in a rush over impenetrable forest
saliva and mucus and desperation of breath the poet
in his frail and puny essence to make a single noise
to be captured by the sonant gold syllables reverberating
in an orchestra of differing silences if only to *understand* !
like leaves swept away in a hurricane iridescent and green
vowels in profusion litter the ineffable aura
goddess , the , *imagination*

lxvii

what will then the poem in meaning be
when morphology and sound-laws lack
but winter's file of driving winds and theory
its stanzas scatter without purpose and
words like swirling snows feckless deviate
from form and love itself a weight on
the divided heart whose memory is one
brief heat in the summer of a single hour
did verses gather of themselves like tresses
of the nymphs bottled in a shimmer green
or leaves imprinted with mind's mad
thoughts of grief and longing and high
too the sun's unremitting orb molds
noon into a statue of merciless oblivion
come then to the other side where rills
argent and pastoral over pebbles glide
and in the spreading shade let life at last
be gone a whim between two bleak nights
the poem its incandescent origins its muse
a shape of beauty only dreams can share
vowel and trailing echo of cliff and vale
threnody casting its distant wail across
the bier and plot and urn of ashes cold
the will to live the timeless ennui of breath
the stubborn hexameter in roiling seas
mist and pearl and eternal fogs errant
melodies and syllables of a remote end
feet deployed over lost hills and yearning
the least ray of the setting lamp a glow
a vanishing before the starry vault
implodes leaving of the poem no sense
punctuations of silence endless sighs
the soul's steep torment and to die
unsigned the burning paper script

lxviii
ascribe these verses to the lovelorn the sick
of heart the variegated shepherd lost on his rock
fuming and repentant that life the years whistled
though his oaten reed you know the story and
exiled from court and with a tattered bag
the contents of a life's worth of versifying
scribbled and deleted and repositioned words
no one has ever heard of and conceits and
skies of angry thunderheads rolling ever west
towards the origins of consciousness and one foot
daintily stepping over the arcadian pond and
the damsel to whom it is attached shall he summon
her to memory or merely echo the echo of her
vision or version a hotel and darkness that
follows the pursuit and envy and its hologram
the witless hours spent penning amorous cantos
only to have running from the wild bushes
Death herself the raving and ravishing in skirts
borrowed from the Dravidian mindset all praise
for the god that created and consumed her
blue throat manic gaze dancing on the Wheel
a hundred thousand collaborations with dead bards
vatic pronouncements about the One and the Shadow
the many who cannot and never did and the force
of destiny and the three-wheeled bike rusting
in the verger and where did she and how did she
going through the windswept stone fragments
the puzzle of the temple erected over night
thirty stories high sculpted with the five million
images of the deity and the alas the forsaken
the picture of the hospital bed the screens the machines
and the coughing and breathless fits *the one I loved*
sitting there noon after noon on his now fading rock
a milligram of sulfur confusion and detritus

of mind the havoc of learning to live for what
days spent in a single hour when years don't matter
the rag tied around the head the ears scorning
all melody and sleep the invisible exterminator
hand over hand the poem rattled and fused and
crumpled and rewritten backwards using a
mirror to realize the fullness of devotion
to her Death the skirted pillaged bag of bones
dancing high and as beautiful as anyone or anything
spangles and beringed fingers and forty bracelets
copper gold beaten silver shaking on her arms
again and again she will take the light and eat it

ascribe these verses to the lovelorn the sick

lxix

an inaudible primordial text
is poetry conscious or does it dwell in the nightscape
aching for the deity whose immense invisibility
confuses the boundaries between space and time
for the godhead it longs for the hand between
the leaves the face hidden in the grass the root
and sheaf of last summer's wheat the ear of the shell
pink and iridescent in the hovering twilight
that exists between thinking and seeing
when everything that was red loses its sound
and only the persistent echo of the cicadas
drowns sleep in its own dark invention
or is poetry just an imperfect memory of heat
of the mountain and its cascades of liquid gold
syllables woven between vowel and vowel
gliding across the parapet where mind hovers
waiting to be performed and forgotten by autumn
a recitation and a circumference around a moon
whose terrific whiteness is the morphology of dreams

or if poetry *is* the end of grammar where is order
where are the shuttle and loom of syntax the click
and stammer the small notches in the unheard note
what is more beautiful than that ? a music before
meaning a melody organized by sand and ink a pyramid
lifting its base to the clouds that write upside down
in the mirror of a metaphorical sky thundering
within the rock that stands formidable and irrelevant
on the edge of the water that composes shadows
mortar and brick of illusion fingers spent
searching for the shape of oblivion and loss
or is poetry finally the unconscious lexicon of the dance
mimicry and silhouette of language before language
feet patterns of diglossia insects a million years old
whatever resists motion at the bottom of the sea
riddles and puzzles and evanescent corporeal images
dying in fact and only dying that is the subject
of poetry the imitation of unspoken unknown words
inky vague repetitions of color and nerve
the eye itself baffled by the enigmatic convexity
that stands before it a wavering smoke ladder
a signal from beyond the periphery of vision
the reverse of glass surface of ether densities
between the male and female parts of the divinity
unspeakable ! everything beyond the gravity of sound
aphonic aphasic numinous vanishing
like black ink from a palm leaf scroll
like north from the map of indifference
like love from the heart of one who has surrendered

lxx

the drunken goddess of poetry
between intoxication and clarity and the dream
of doing business with demons or ghouls

the goddess in all her raiment of celestial ether
seraphic of voice climbing increments of sky
thrusting off advances by kings and merchants
chanted and stung by poets of imperfection
she herself the twenty-six vowels of the ineffable
struggles to wake and her maidens the sirens
of watery depths and the dancers and barmaids
who wait on her every whim like a swarm of bees
mired in their own sweet froth try to return her
to a level of consciousness known only to gods
the great oracle of the rock formation sends
its enormous and invisible utterances forth
a chariot comprised of the consonants of fire
horses of adulation and devotional sweat
exude an impatience for the battles of teleology
and memory and all around there are dust storms
angelic deserts of unending ennui and lace
and they sprinkle libations of mead and barley
over the parts of her skin most adapted to melody
and the song which is the integral part of her delta
coruscations of unwritten letters loud and sweet
almost the entire text of a veda in praise of hair
leaves of sybilline devastation rustle their tongues
reciting in the whispered monotones of the dead
verses culled from the voyage south of time
many are the silences the retrograde illusions
of life on earth of nerve and shell and grasses
that rush like oceans across the various infancies
of the goddess when with lotus feet and fevered
by the taste of nard and hyacinth and hands
that tattooed the winds with gorgeous lyrics
inspirations of beauty and longing she danced
high on the mountain tops and spurned suitors
and promised herself to no one but the *Other*
and today ! drunk out of her dulcet mind

buoyed by her already wasted retinue and night
that selfish thief of thoughts descends taking what
remains of her mentation and in a swirl of silks
and velvets and the tossing about of palms and beads
she revives momentarily shameless in a mere
turquoise loin wrap-around her gaze wildly pivoted
on the bird's-eye target that no hero can pierce
she becomes more than a goddess more than
what mortals can sustain in their brief experience
she becomes withheld breath anima of light
the thing that demands an origin since she has none
the dizzy spinning flight out of control
through the myriad spheres of consecutive
and parallel eternities the inaudible ululation
that reduces space to a single witless and insane syllable
she has come forth from her addiction
the face and nothing more of unremembered *love*

lxxi

verses clouds scudding through a loophole of air
the bathers in all their mystery missing loves
and mourning losses from another life a tempest
to be borne and the recitation of the names of Nymphs
Drymo Xantho Ligea Phyllodoce Nisaee and Cydippe
the blond Licorias and Thalia and sister Beroë
from islands below the sea their fanciful unkempt hair
and bracelets amulets and jewels pawned for the god
who sits high on an emerald pedestal to judge with
but one eye the vain and mortal follies far below
where I came by a radio invisible and loud playing
cities by the number and between the quoits and
flying digits a sample of sorrow I heard them play
lyrics and voices torn from leaves and ghosts
of lovers in their cortical disbelief returned once

more to shed their tears in groves and grottoes
fashioned by a poet and lofty pinnacles of distance
the mountain where was hid an enigmatic truth
the quandary of ego and masks that do not fit souls
in their prison-house of being and error the tryst
of evenings in miasma and amber legendary lone
specters in an effort to recognize the one who went
before simplex and circumstance of a lighted day
forever gone if only one could remember why
the radio so loud so faraway shadows of Nymphs
their names like mountain rills and echoes shy
to the sleeper buried in his dream of stone

lxxii

a! miseram Eurydicen anima fugiente vocabat:
Eurydicen toto referebant flumine ripae.
*   Virgilus, Georgicon IV, 526-527*

from Virgil we get news this morning to grieve
not just Eurydice involved thrice by eternal night
but Philomela and other shades as well Philomela
on her branch bewailing her rent tongue and
whistles and beads and laments on painted shells
the whole surge of the under-waters black that
nine times circle the Stygian deep and more than
that my sorrow to multiply in marmoreal tones
who last seen in pitiful hospital gown lay still
before the yawning abyss and the Eumenides
in raiment of fiery clouds took him up ululating
and the nymphs of wood and dale and the rocks
to whom I make appeal and the radio with its
suborned voices of secret catastrophe in song
and haunting melody and stone and crescent
moon the diadem of obfuscated silver glow
and places without name where I have been before

a shadow casting shadow on the moving rills
and earth I took to be a grave mistake and gyres
of words that make no sense the whole paraphernalia
the circles a false illumination in the bottom sky
for there are no answers in the mourning groves
nor fingers pleading alphabets of the grasses
that once teemed in summer's single afternoon
a kite a boy a pale reflection in the doorway
some soil rubbed against the tinder box a match
a small flare before immense time through its
window enters to rob all of sight and sound
the world ! some syllables a stray vowel echoes
and nothing more whom I grieve this Wednesday
as on all days dedicated to Mercury and
when fever took his voice away

Tityre, te patulae cecini sub tegmine fagi.
       Georgicon IV,566

lxxiii

as gravity unfolds and the circular letters
lose themselves in flight towards some supernal order
seas mount their siege on land and air
gathers into knots of wind unleashing tempests
rains of forty floors years encapsulated in a thimble
there is no precision to memory the Muses teach
dying to the grasses and whoever sleeps among them
children transmogrified by an electric spark
and the dark chambers where mind seeks light
but never obtains it and the small information
about the gods whose job is to wrack and ruin
whatever was placed on the altar whatever smoked
with incense and piety whatever flared in thought
of renewal and sacrifice only the bones of a text
flayed remnants of a song about skin

tendentious thunder about to roll through the ear
and stone and rock and failed masonry of temples
where was the error which was the path not taken
and the unexpected deaths the grieving trees
by the roadside and the dry wells and the names
half pronounced half unsaid meant to propitiate
why we exist on this planet with our cattle and hills
and rhododendron and hyacinth and hellebore
the palace shining with crystal and sundown
we stand before it shaking with premonition
sleep extends its greater hemisphere of inks
over the western peninsula where we disappear
one by one forgotten to each other bidden to end
in separate vowels fading in search of an echo
cliff and surf and bottomless water on the other side
where myth and recurrence of time vanish

lxxiv

to whom address the next letter the torn page
the quartered paragraph the symbiotic lichen
vanquished in a history of misinterpretations
under glass versifications and denunciations
clicking hissing steaming in mid-air the sibyl
pleading the cause of crystal and rust watching
far-off cities diminish in the corporate shadow
of the mountain and who are playing in circles
a dance of nymphs corrupted by alphabets and
the nuisance of language sounding brass and high
in winds loud with ruin and prophesies the world
will be no better wave and salt and vengeance
of ions and photons the immense halt of the day
noon stilled with its breathing marble horses
to address these imperfections of thought this
stillborn red in its cradle of printed leaves wild

and unassuaged by the promise of water in drops
distilled from a rock hanging over the entrance
to Avernus nearby shores plangent with memory
of shipwreck and hiatus and the huge Greek Zeta
blocking the wharf and the impounded skiffs and
the blind messengers smashing squid against the wall
who will come to terms with what this has to say
and in a dialect broken like the symbols employed
by Dante and the invisible flight of birds archaic
in wingspan and bewailing in stygian syllables
who will come to this punctuation of the deaf
that reckon with drugged hands meter and rhyme
not being of this world but of the imagined blackboard
where are conjugated the verbs to *be* and to *die*
dust bins of mown grass withering yellow in the fade
of a late byzantine afternoon the apostolic virtues
declaimed in hoarse tones ornaments defiled and
whomever else this letter will not address coming
from behind the hill and trees bitter with recondite
knowledge of the unspoken route and the hemorrhage
in the heavens roiling thunder and acid-storms
finish it ! ideograms sculpted in sand and basalt
a pharaonic light beneath the river eerie glowing
to signal to the dead it's time and some reborn as
animals panther or gazelle able to communicate
what they saw in the previous life and doctors
wearing flashlights to probe foot- and fingerprints
left in the mud that seals the oracle in its utterance
tomorrow is a trumpet a splintered sound a note
so distant that none will ever wake again to it
phrase and fuse and required signature at the
bottom of this unaddressed unwritten letter

lxxv

> ed io ero ghiotto
> d'amore ancora
> malgrado i miei anni
> E. Pound, Canto LXXIII

greedy for love despite my years unsure which
house which hearth which abandoned domain
to enter pleading to illegible gods for a reference
a path a sign a pebble white not black to assure
the route underground and back Proserpina's
lithe ivy swift hand on my shoulder and turning
to the scent of cigarettes on her breath and to see
the instantaneous flare in her eyes all spell and
incantation bringing the moon down rising sea-level
drowning the fabulous lacustrine cities of dream
it was in the colophon the et cetera of a paraphrase
of love of the incidents notched into the revolving
wheel the mountain and its opposite lifted heavy
with shadow and the evening vowels a cascade of
song rills of the unconscious as she hugged me
squeezing me so tight light of day fled my mind
eager for love for a caress from her blanched *being*
it was not backwards it was not a mirror nor a
glass left on the blackened wild shoreline nor even
the infinity of a single syllable uttered on her lips
plaintive and mourning it was the lack of years
remaining the small wharf at the tip of echo
something to cling to a cliff a resonance of gold
wavering like a shroud over the Beloved's face
hazy and distant yet in the very here and now
the whole of the abyss turned upside down and
skirts and hair and bracelets jangling and grass
everywhere in the mouth and nostrils and green
the planets fleeing in their enigmatic conspiracy

what was to know ? hungry for love in my advanced
years a thin horizon cutting night in half a thread
almost invisible separating life from death

lxxvi

and Mira Bai marveled wondering what was truth
you must go to Brindaban to find Krishna at play
on the Agra-Delhi highway lush hills fetid heat groves
can all that has been before be cancelled so easily ?
the quick light of the earliest day and monsoon threat
everything colored purple a rush of showers elephants
chains and a tyrant in his tower waiting vengeance
what are the souls of children and to be squandered
in a blind thrust at fame and enormous sand and ivy
curling around the waists of thirty-three thousand brides
a mountain is only so great the rest are dancing girls
ephebes full blown in embroidered silk and lacquer
how can a mind best display its errant dreams ?
to invent poetry repeatedly starting with invocations
to the sun and one day you will grow up and see
through these forgeries issued as bank statements
or truisms of commerce and grain settlements and
given a map of the stars will thirst for something more
subtle for the heavens are artificial as are the numbers
that compose them and know there are only the verses
without count unfinished and seeking renewal as
a Christ laid below the stone is promised a third hour
and ignorance and its foil history that abound among
sterile rock and what can you make of the mirage
of cities built one upon the other and toppled like
match sticks or put to the flame like onion skin paper
does one ever wake again beside deep pools to hear
above in the branches of a banyan the melancholy
shriek of the peahen and to bring down the tempests

looking in the rills and byways for some trace of brother
the orient which was setting in his eyes the last time
when noon folded up its parapet and maps and aloud
the skyless clouds seemed to languish in a colored lens
Mira Bai still an adolescent in love with a statuette
married to the icon of the blue-skinned boy her fever
a brain with inherent vowels attached to consonants
the trip to Brindaban and the *sufis* and *Naths* like
a cyclone of inner powers reciting in a trance eternal
the unidentified non-dual self and then an implosion
of red powders destroys the concrete world its paths
and jungles and terrorists and on the other side
of the language of silence rise the multiple levels
of light the shattered lamp the intoxicated spark
fireflies in the myriads devouring human thought
++
Mira Bai

lxxvii

the thread in its force like the lion's
fixity of mind phosphorous and gold
the tawny sun high in the mid hour
stone against stone grass underneath
seeking a lamp a sure bright fierce
that cuts through glare and mist alike
and sea gold-tipped its waves brings
to the godlike shore sharp and creased
as thought fresh from its sleeping lair
a man a finger withheld a cloud-image
drifting through polished glass paradise
in the least amount and the bay roaring
in the rock's adamant ear by dark a
softened element by grief brought down
to bear upon the smaller heavens that
protrude upon the historical event a city

a green metropolis of emerald memory
sitting upon the mysterious oracle that
invented it the mouth of the sleeper a
sibylline accent the trees on either side
eucalyptus or willow and the salt embryo
buried deep within the unuttered vowel
will all this come around and when again
the switch is flipped and into relief come
the persons of the masque and a music
of oboe and tambourine the felt sound
of feet without pattern and the cliff carved
from a painting at the end of the sky
what of the embroidered hues in the eye
the siren in the ear the cadavers left
to mourn in Circe's littered precinct a
war among unseen chthonic deities a
raised syllable among chattering leaves
desperation it is remembering manhood
down *there* among printed silks and icons
of the Mother-of-God fluttering lachrymose
the abyss and its counterpart the high note
unsounded brilliant weft in the skies
Orion falling down with great sadness
and the Pleiades with their rain color
of distance come the dawn and its ash
turning to rose the multiple rebirths
panther becomes stag and stag leans
against wind to learn the Pythagorean
secret the triangle and the mimosa
something comes of nothing and a hand
holding a brush sketches eternity
in a small pink thumbnail ere evening
brings a chill to spine and mind lists
into the least flaw of indigo night
lost forever

lxxviii

"in short shall we look for a deeper or is this the bottom?"
E. Pound, Canto LXXIV

arcadia not being sufficient enough a garden
to the other side of the hill pushing southwards
to where they say the dead embroider eyelids
with sleep we went tarrying with broken compass
below the signs of the Water-Carrier or Scorpion
who addressed us in the fractured Italian of inferno
setting sail in mind only for ports of heat and memory
midday found us stranded in mud and with the sound
of leaves restless in the idiom of Dionysus rustling
profound in the backwaters where no man has yet set
foot realizing in the heights of the pale draining sky
the least of us the soul of a child or a butterfly dazed
circling the fraction of given air the light but a re-
flection and the antipodes and the loud gear of
mariners ensnared in their own riggings hapless
and without an alphabet to guide and the tempests
predicted for the third watch already whirling yellow
dust cataracts bullion of the sun in sulfuric mists
raining down over the expanse of distant seas
earth no more a reality than the hand in its design
to take back from the past the myth of resurrection
owl and gibbet and rotting timber lyesol and arsenic
to pull down from the rafters the skeletons of stars
the debris and bric-a-brac of an archaic language
speaking to us in metaphors of silk and dissolution
the *manes* shadow entities of a broken Rome and marble
lifted from the depths set upright and began to talk
spirals of old flame and halos of dysentery and rust
the air stifling with the cognition of man's brevity
lies and malware and brute recensions of *Paradiso*
what was to go the extra the last mile sand mounds

ant heaps a mountain rearing its sudden menace
a minute and it was a litter of frenzied dialects
poetries of salvation reincarnation and non-duality
wherever a finger could point the illegible beauty
shimmering apostasy in the wavering cloud buff
directing a chorus of silences and otherness a wild
Antarctic illusion of the afterlife draped in whites
blanched tertiary notions of love and unending !
beyond this stillpoint this punctuation of fans
and empty rooms cabins tilted into space yawning
cavities where to lay the head down stone and ice
and listen ! the dizzying bees of afterthought
seeking and never finding their Mount Hybla
beyond this stillpoint *what ?*

lxxix

we are to address *La Romana* in her 16th year
debutante with automotive hair slick black
cinematic exile in back lots and parking cruisers
stiletto heels and bright rouge incarnadine mouth
lip gloss and ivory smooth forehead wrinkled
ever so slightly a question mark a virtual reality
transmogrified endowed with insect intelligence
winged and vibrating in a coruscating sun
half-life of heat pornographic glyph of the Pharaohs !
it is tomorrow with her every day the section
of red that incorporates violence and humility
a Pietà of the post-war suburbs a decoration
taken from the sleep of the Twelve Caesars
intaglio and dialect murmuring underworld buzz
paparazzi on every corner flashing bulbs loud
and incriminations even before adolescence is over
poetry written in marble schemes of infinity
sensation of headlines and necrologies and above

all volcanic activity constantly in motion irregular
verb and indentation of air increasing Sicily
as it heads for landing in Campo Santo AOI !
she is she is she is *la Romana Ragazza Puella*
divine comedy *Trionfo d'amore* syzygy and madness
combs and reticulations of saliva a wantonness
in search of Byzantium skirts and wildflowers
azure on azure painted lavender to resemble
the Tyrrhenian sea in the crepuscular hour
eyelids dotted with fragrances of the Pleiades
Paestum and Herculaneum both above and below
ground and the winnowing inches of soil and mud
where Proserpina celebrates her Nth birthday !
weeping and joyous both that light has a reversal
and the sudden and open night come to devour
the shadows of men still talking on ramparts
of war and profit to which *La Romana* turns
her back revealing the moon's shimmering posterior
lunations and gravity and ascension *Annunziata* !
today we are come with offerings to lay on the altar
prayers and wheels and small decibels of delight
insane   proclivities to transcend the Self forever
will she or will she not glance our way ?

lxxx

the forms of heat and columns of air lifting
from earth's dream of Alexander and Central Asia
silk routes and ox-cart courses newly carved
from the weft of error // inscriptions in Brahmi
succor the poor relief to the sick wayside taverns
barley mons veneris spoon and umbrella all
relate to the consonant inside the man and the vowel
which stands for woman and what arises
trembling in the noon's unilateral shimmering

yoni and nirvana and the illiterate desert of sleep
things that remain after the flood and tempest
even sun is a remnant of the greater lamp
a poem found in the recesses of space and illumined
dipththongs and virtues of a shelf listing above
water all in italics and fed to the intellectuals
of colonialism and let them rave about progress
future in a set of stilted letters cut into stone
hazard a guess the emblem unfolds and a child
issue of grass and hologram the illness being
born risen to the height of a midpoint glyph
standing as it were on the fountain of desire
not recognizing the ephemeral window
fan-palm circle a bow the eye gathered in a mesh
spelled and reiterated as the afternoon *Gong* !
resounds sending ripples through crystal
and what of the dead who have been shunted south
in alphabetical coffins a lair of cave and mint
the sky a hundred names for the ever-after
that has no echo and bilateral coruscations of moon
the goddess in a slip of see-though skin walking
through the mountain of passion unfeeling
who will bear as *Kwanon* an infant and weeping
over its fate and unable to read what is on its brow
a finger and a leaf and the slowly moving film
eleven faces a thousand hands Mercy drifting across
the trance of breath and peak after peak
of snow and glistening was ever the end so near ?
ruin cultivated for the vanishing beauties of memory
and its daughters of rain and cloud mist
distance itself imprinted on the passing ledger
ear serpent and sickle signifying an enclosure
the quadrilateral face of Brahma inscrutably turning
as the female element which is origin and conclusion
goes through the ideograms of thought phantom

borne of dust and the rose footsteps over silk
whispers inaudible litany of the stars

lxxxi
it's the first thing to use grammar
and learn as butterflies to wing it
talking the sound of flutter and flurry
you are a child only so long and chalk
held nimbly to color the sky's board
fragments of letters the frieze of breath
old you'll become one sad day the hour
when of a sudden something happens
and the anthology with its task of leaf
and branch the appendage to thought
a flowering in bloom of time the hues
alive with air the racing fast across a
single consonant held on the tongue
syllabic quantity becomes important
like the red of the unique vowel shown
on the verso of the last page of school
when it's the bell and over the sadder
yet to not come home to lie there below
the sun's glaring eye with number as
a serial fiction in your head a mind
to overcome heat and decibels ringing
in the brain quaint echoes riverrun
argent rills drilled in the faint ear
head of stone it could be or grass in
its last possibility winnowing memory
out of the wind setting down a finger
at a time the reference to antiquity
the temple ruin half on its side half lost
in the photograph where it darkens a
night on the Aegean it says in scribbled

hand a pillow for an accent and the sea
in fierce rushing takes by surprise the
land at its behest and heroes on the verge
multiply their cries against fate savage
hoops played by the gods you have learnt
and tried to understand and within the
child you were the versifying angel
broken in two by life's unexpected knee
glass in its entirety upended released
into the pool of stars to imitate and be
imitated the saddest of all reflections
cocoon you have been now it's over
dusty wings slanting into the flame
light passing over light *gone*

lxxxii
what has happened in the last ten thousand years ?
will we ever really know who killed the Kennedys ?
the taxidermist takes the sun as a trophy of the hunt
while the goddess of the Chase turned to plaster falls
to ruin even as she races light to the forest clearing
in museum corridors paintings dialogue between hues
of consciousness and the shattered rosary of history
to question Pound in his polyglot eloquence and set
up row after row of sling shot and target practice
on the mural of the body politic igniting the schoolyard
with justification of the 2nd Amendment and to desire
to go to the Moon or Mars ignoring the unshod illiterate
in deserts overrun by Jihad and nation-state fanaticism
what is rising sea-level to Opera house millionaires ?
take apart piece by piece the chapters of Edward Gibbon
buffoon and illustration of Byzantine opacity and
suddenly it's the Renaissance or Song Dynasty glory
big boats exploring the wild seas and gunpowder and print

shall we return to the deer-park where Vedanta unfolds
in sheet after sheet of light and the quiet of mind float
in an unspoken Nirvana and forty thousand Arhats
implode in a teakwood ministry of salvation and bliss ?
rapid-fire rap of drug driven automobiles resounding
monochrome hagiography of gossip slander and drivel
the trivial raised to the Nth degree and celestial boudoirs
slashed by technology and even faster gigabytes *Ahoy !*
tomorrow is no sooner yesterday then noon-time hits
all time stock market high and et cetera gilded in fake
and pallid imitations of absolutely nothing and illegal
to boot the borders stiffen and increase with despotic hate
barbed wire intaglios of gesso saints painted with booze
worshipped by kneeless and hooded vagrants from
the south where the dead are harvested by dictators
whose pedigrees extend back to penniless Conquistadors
the world is fast becoming its own coffin ready for cremation
children ! it is time to *unlearn* the lessons of democracy !

what has happened in the last ten thousand years ?
will we ever really know who killed the Kennedys ?

lxxxiii
(adieu)
lotus dream honey suckle,
where've you been all my life ?
traces of your feet fleeing
from the cave and ivy whistle
green around your tiny ears
like shells pink as moon asleep
waves of passion songs of loss
that are gone before the light
everything seems to stop when
grass turns the bottomless
afternoon into running seas

a link a ribbon a lip of gloss
each time you switch your waist
or lift a finger to tip an ivory scale
world goes dumb and drowns
inside the rose's labyrinthine dew
and me I'm tossed about from
life to life breathless smoking wild
your mouth a wounded distance
that separates planets of memory
from the thing I most desire
space darkens in the missing eye
and sleep revolves its myth
inside the number of your mind
how can I ever knew whether
you are shape or simply air
no hand can revive or hold
phantom lamp of reverie
Arcadia of the long unseen
gyre of heat and inconstancy
you were what should never be
woman of beguiling death
vowel of endless symmetry
dwelling deep within the leaf

lxxxiv

should have known the process coming to an end
when breath in revulsion and the tattered air
the signals sent from the raving eye the time
is come to close the cloud and shutter out the wind
machines only have so much electricity the body
a rent and disheveled cloth dangling on the line
to spin a future out of dust and soil loose figments
the mind in disarray and light a spark of memory
released from the shattered beam the gods in rout

each to their rock relent unspoken their former beauty
a marble in halves divided twenty times by fifty
the vacant bottom of the ocean's floor a vast shell
of reiterated echoes that come back no more
islands and sunsets and cliffs eroded by nature's
fierce desire to suicide how many beginnings and
all for naught the useless entity of mind a presage
it should have been when the ambulance turned
the wrong direction and streets flew backwards
into a map of childhood's long missing vowels
you ask I know why I still grieve a fistful of ashes
a thin streak zigzagging across the gathered lawn
a balloon a sphere a kite let go above the solemnity
brick and diapason and stairs that only descend
all hells are in the empty inch and steaming Cocytus
revolves its inky coils around the house of hours
where we still dwell among littered consonants
torn from a machine that writes necrologies and odes
cannot return nor ever will again the fragility sweet
the softness of that now absent wound a life sewn
within a dream of leaves that stain the air with green
a springtime once ! a hill of distances sublimely bright
hand and knee and focus on the spinning sun
whose transient flares illumined now darkened earth
a sleep a night a thing that has lost its process
disappearing in the endless folds of space

lxxxv

"Quanto hoc furiosius atque
maius peccatum est"
Horatius

Zagreus !   Meat !   Inferno !
incoherence of religious texts
analogy of the beast strangled by ivy

and sacred things stolen from the temple
at night when the garden is exposed
trampled underfoot by the holy Thief
and the invisible but burning angel
denying entrance to everyone on Sundays
look down into the stony abyss
transfiguration of number and mood
loud as the distance between sun and Pluto
louder than the last thought ever recorded
Atlantis ! Polyphemus ! let fly the rocks
into the wake of nostalgic waters
parasites of Rome ! swine of Circe !
leaves that can see inside the soul
a poem that unwinds from the root
darkness and the story of *Osiris*
a thousand and one bits scattered
over the wet planetarium floor
and the word for blood bandied about
from spear tip to spear tip and high
and swift the rook and raven winging it
frenzied cloud with inchoate voices
dappled silver steeds dashing over the cliff
Hesperides untranslated ! mansions of light
ignition of all cuneiform vowels
macron and circumflex and hydrangeas
silence that comes in circles sleeping
and grass and more grass *Adonis !*
profanation of the venereal consonants
how to choose which one to sacrifice ?
who will wield the eleatic knife ?
possibility of motion ! speed ! loss !
matter comes into being just as
space disappears in sleight of hand
children become kites without string
a god hands them a rope and they fly

right into the serpent's eye !
holy ! holy ! holy ! Minerva undressed !
it is always too late for breath to return
and memory ! mist travels over mist
fireflies take possession of the museum
marble mouths ! a notion to die !

lxxxvi
Coatlicue
winding down the cicatrix hush among ivy
clambering up the shattered ruin a wall
in the ear a fixed night in the eye a fragment
of song and skin the deathless wish to die !
Mercury's silent car races infinity to the end
a contest between the German twins reason
and madness and furious atomic clouds
orange to the point of purity destroy the cosmos
a dream between two blades of grass and
a leaf placed carefully in a Chinese saucer
a fortune to withhold a future to white out
blank the mind blanker still its very thought
children I ask who have never existed drawing
their locomotive toys and spinning coils
where have they gone where is their sleep
abode in mountains of a single dust and
storms in the iris of the painted coffin
flowers of error blooms iridescent and wild
nights come and go letting no day in between
an hour in the lapsed code of language
a minute before the next universe begins
this myth we write with mechanical fingers
playing pianos of abstract matter and loud
the meaning and its counterpart aphasia
vowels we string together consonants that

have nowhere to go a violent soundless rain
a fragrance of gardens denied to all
we list this way and that on paper rafts
adrift on seas beyond ink's cold margins
a god of stone that struts weightless in his
unmapped sky color in reverse clouds heavy
with the antecedent of melody fission and fugue
alternation of moon and muse in bedlam
afternoons locked inside a tri-dimensional window
waiting for the cup and horse
a spirit world within a phantom
pyramid a porch a storm of fireflies
the goddess *Coatlicue* come to eat her fill
of night and the starry afterworld

lxxxvii
1949

the light fled from the tops of the trees
and disappeared into the sky
how old were we then ? and the color
passing into the hills from ripe gold
to ocher dun and echo of red and something
of the mystery of vanishing like sleep
in leaves darkening at the onset of gloom
smoke traces trailing letters into the night
when the first stars could be counted
then becoming innumerable for us
as for Ulysses adrift in his own memory
a call from the trunks blackening in the park
or the rippling rill of the nearby stream
walking home in all of that a tangle
of lives and messages from unknown pasts
to learn of the seed and lay the ear into it
moon far above cancelling the latest hour

before the tremendous vision of the house of Thunder
where plotting with wheel and compass the director
of the gods prepared fates for each of us
a prophesy of years unraveling in pyramids
dust and orients of fabulous crystal
roseate at the beginning then flush spreading
downwards as we got nearer to the approach
of Hades not far from the schoolyard
empty of its silhouettes and shadows
down even further beyond the realm of sound
into the workings of the dream-source
pale effigies playing with scout-knives
redrawing the borders of maps depths
of peril and longing and error
which is the way of the world above
the threading and beading of thoughts
and language symbols that arise from silence
interwoven in the fabric of space the scintillating
waiting finally in the dark counting on the wall
the headlight beams of passing cars
wondering when mother would get home
whether she was still stranded in a room
enormous for its distance from time
enigma and miscomprehension
of why we were anything at all
like dumb ruminating beasts
peering into dewy fields of grass
at the break of still another
irreversible *dawn*

lxxxviii

what is recovered ? nothing
what is observed ? nothing
history written inside a sleeve

that releases wind and skies
blown away by noon and still
the disorder the angst the vowel
placed in the midst of air gathered
for a ceremony of instances outside
the time-zone and memories
are passed about with gloves
the trees listen intently it is
their season of gold and green
and the secrets of the cave
and the grotto and the mountain
the sidelined cliffs and roaring
sea-violence down below and
for once the poem uncataloged
left to wither in the purple sun
of the initiates of Pythagoras
climbing inches higher toward
the folio with its lexical dross
the librarian pitches a code
and light breaks forth from
the one volume left to dry
after Ulysses has gotten home
and the banners flying on the left
summon the Chinese pirates
with their walkie-talkies and
glass automobiles and the world
we once thought to be a puzzle
now resembles an anemone
a colored bauble a fragile toy
dropped from the hand
of the child denied the justice
of life and breath a fever
the shaking idiom of illusion
words travel so fast over
the sheets of ink and never

stay put long enough
to read them right

lxxxix

what is understanding of the world ?
morning-glory seed or posterity of a rain drop
effluvia of the mind fallen into its arroyo
and the thousand dawns that encumber it
a plane flying the wrong direction
right into a sun-spot a flare as great as an ant
the eye as it turns outside in to recognize
the depths the darkness the endlessness
before birth the timelessness after death
a finger gone from each hand and grass
in the multitudes sweeping shadows away
laying the head down on stone to listen
for the untrammeled excavation of light
not understanding not thinking not talking
only the puzzled vowel of aphasia
pronounced as if it were the one sacred text
and between you and me there is a secret
a mysterious conflagration a terrible memory
that all Tuesdays coincide with Wednesday
that there is no way out of the rock
where sleep binds us to a mutual dream
that we will never know one another !
there is a bed and a siphon and a wall
writing that comes and goes in snatches
of ideogram and cuneiform and pyramids of salt
dissolving in the long punctuations of water
where boats list in search of liquid gold
of the crevice from which riches of thought
pour intangible and evanescent
a music a raiment of shimmering air

and clouds which are the theory of steam
come to naught evidence of insanity
and anarchy and tenderness in the void
where children are put to rest from surfeit
of reason and as always the lawns
that extend into eternity a distance
unfolded in the span between thumb and index
the world ! what is to understand ?
antiquity of the unheard sound !

xc

how many sizes does it take to wear a year ?
and the number of grief when you call long distance ?
forty nine floors up is what divided by what ?
to measure the quantity of dactyls in a given hue
is there enough metaphor to cross the ocean ?
does a statue live for a monument only
or for all the unconsecrated hours of antiquity ?
is the leaf torn from its branch loss of voice
or merely diminishment of echo ?
the ear ! conflagrations of intimate vowels
retroflex consonants on the wane as moon rises
in ruddy splendor displaying a submarine face
womankind ! Helen Cassandra and Klytemnestra
hands of blood and love trysts inside the Trojan rock
severed from all tenderness the nerve in its hiatus
imitates nothing less than the heavens plunged
into a *Purgatorio* of allegory and machine parts
is the number three the certainty of another life ?
is it the leg or the shoulder in which prayers
at the root of all archaic discourse occur ?
temples in ruin abandoned fountains trills of lark
and nightingale the force of *Destiny !*
and yet and yet and yet moss is an attribute

to tragedy clinging to a forlorn and abject tree-trunk
and the blackening of the sun by high noon
and the fiercely devout syllable at the entrance
to the green-house where the corpse of Achilles
lies in state bathed wept and reviled for his flowering
and when the rocket fuel runs out and the thumb
in its trajectory fails to sign then and only then
will the cloud-buffer separate thought from silence
igniting the mansions where alphabets of the gods
give shape to literature and the myth of oblivion ?
memory ! the other side of glass or the reverse of light ?
everything subsumed in the minute it takes
to form questions about eternity and dying

xci

and not far from that hole which is the entry
to the great and dark under-space we played
innocent of reflection and inwit bathed in light
but as the hours passed and turned night inside out
and the hills and crannies of distance evolved
into a myth we too grew remote as the hand is
from the shoulder in the aging process and to
know one another was a thing of the past a tale
played out by nymph and rock and sparkling fount
the edges of time and space coalesced and music
the mind intensified in the puzzle to understand
itself and snatches of language came and went
drilling the earhole with buzz and consonant
like the speech of mandarins or bees in echoes
that passed from leaf to leaf and to actually *know*
to distinguish day from day and the revolving
receipt of activities orders issued from heaven
the gods themselves in amusement clambering
in clouds and trees and spearing to the death

whom they adored we watched the highways
become littered with dear souls and longing
the sometimes furious loss of body and memory
it was life to call it a higher sense of motion
seeds of thought inarticulate and in dialect
a form of speed and the length of shadows
by noon and the long slow endgame of stone
the forgetting and only the shapes of grass
ebbing toward some inexplicable twilight
turning to look one of us was already missing
and the tears because we had to cry the grief
and not sudden but nevertheless total darkness

xcii

the forgetting yes so hard to do
the illusory passage of days when
it is only the one minute that counts
when it happened and never again
driving around in a god-driven vehicle
and radio blasting and still the native air
the fossil winds the skeletal sky the clouds
in their looming claustral formations
ink and the spilled sluice of the stars
even at noon masquerading as Nemesis
thin bilateral asterisk endowed with speed
and the fiery likeness to memory
sudden as everything really is without
the consciousness of accident or grammar
the will to exist ! we can number them
as high as we want the vowels wanton
and vague and to pronounce a mountain
or slide down the other direction of time
a history of cities inhabited by sleep
and the conjunction and the particle

and the fuselage of syntax exploded
at the root where grass and leaf search
for their etymologies a given myth
to have been born given a name and
collateral weight and the frail attempt
to levitate as well as to collapse breathing
the remnants of what was seen in passing
through anatomical structures called
person or mask and the dance and ballad
sweeping the hair back for a mirror
and stepping forth only to realize
there is no going back only the descent
to that obscure and labyrinthine inch
where night gathers her skirts

xciii

a heat wave at the gates of hell
inches from the gasoline pump
shivered rock and slate that seem
to sing ! or is it light from the bone
and sifting through channels of air
memory on its invisible moon-shaped craft
aloft the fingers of missing children
the enormous hiatus left behind
when the piece of chiseled marble
knocked from its tenement began to
orate in its somnolent buzzing language
keeping the ear close to the stone
that blocks entry to further conclusions
a hand mired in its own text
feet that perpetuate their hesitation
and the nearby underbrush the potential
flame about to take branch by branch
the system of speech and writing and

tossed into the nearby ditch fossils
of thought and dialogue in hieratic tones
of sand the great conveyor and scattered
like puzzles in the wind other voices
cast about looking for rooms to bed
the weary and fugitive soul at a loss as
to what its shape and hue and size should be
a coloratura aria breathed out by the
golden haired soprano in Tuscan
feeling each sculpted crevice each step
the descent and the dark that spreads
its ovarian inks across the stairs
echo follows echo ever downward
even as mind beseeches the infernal gods
for a last remembrance a small flicker
from the sun's waning lamp
it is to sleep beside these ruins
pronouns become useless in their sound
the *I* and the *thou* abandoned
withered leaves and nothing more
shaking in the immense silence
that issues from foregone earth

xciv

and I saw shapes limpid and crystalline
passing through midair forms borrowed
from previous lives shadow and manifest
wings whirred in my ears an obelisk set
upright in the spur of my eye and written
over and over on it massive script furrowed
like a deity's brow and angry and responsive
to the hulk and hasp of tumultuous memory
avenues of shop glitter and heat corrosion
buildings amputated at the fifth floor and

cries and shrieks of secretaries and bellboys
camels with ornate saddle bags and crusts
of air dense with honey of the orient I saw
and felt in the nerve of my left hand a tool
driven deep into the heart and laughter
bound to a small insect maddened by red
the color of distance and longing madness
to recur in sleep and embrace as close to
the breast the hidden statuettes of love
painted and swarming the brain at least
slowly adrift in its own pronoun the egress
and height of a peculiar and tight vowel
ascendant of the other side of the sky
irreversible glass monochrome consonant
smooth opaque as the Nile on a moonless
night summers and the catastrophe of dirt
bereft of its cliff and wandering vagrant stars
aleph and beth and gimel running through
a single flame the proportion of ink as it
weighs on the scales beside the pharaonic *Eye*
a cavity to behold as well I did that moment
a supreme thrill the edge of space a brick
held against its syllable and the terremoto
sea-break crashing tunnels in the fire pit
omicron and gesso spirits flying amok wild
with the spent fascination of pre-birth
will it ever come back this vision phantoms
of the ego ! plural aspects of hair and silk
residency in earth's hiatus where tragedy
and suffix combine to plead grief for all
to end each in the shell of one's conviction
a car hauled by milk-white mules upwards
toward the mountain of sound and when
convex distributions of grass and the worm
in its mulch and the foliage talking wildly

in four different tones the breadth of an hour
exhausted and dream the dense portico when
fireflies wrap their rope around a cigarette
and the girls come running out of a screen
banging hoarse their asterisks upon turf
soft as the again of motion without time
so I saw them passing out of smoke into
a career of wheels stone and rock heights
waving their figures of waist and number
a tremolo swift and echoing and I fainted
as one dead to the spirit fade and null
dark cipher unconscious twin of zero

xcv

the people upstairs never did come down again
the floor the ceiling the winches and stumbling
music of rafters gone wrong and window sealing
to keep endless winter's death out a fraying
nerve a claustrophobic inch of light seeping through
glass and wax wrappers sorrow the uppermost
if we never see their photographs again or
sound the base of their footfalls and the stairs
leaning against a frame of unwritten poetry
they weren't the best their defects were cosmic
they had incidental chasms deformations of character
as ego goes theirs was a wanton disregard for
boundaries improprieties their illustrations
awkward or even pornographic of saints' lives
medieval bestiaries limestone kilns of secrets
hasty conjectures as to the fictions of heaven and
the stiletto in the back the knave of hearts the ace
whose queen subjected the top of the house to riots
all in crimson or red sashes and livery and violent
at times the apogee of a vowel uncontained and holy

discourse in the circularity of heat a nation-state
the size of a stamp was theirs to rule for a day
and a half by noon just smoldering embers a fake
tissue and comb to play the anthem only to weep
because the imprint and the hospital ambulance
stopped by once too many their remains covered
in ornate winding sheets yellowing despair crying
into kerchiefs and prayers to Vishnu or Shiva
never knew which dancing wildly like that on
a small winding top dizzying effect of life
just like that gone ! whiz buzz and instants
later the ringing stopped the ear filled with
stone and the bees outside puzzled as to direction
the trees enormous shaking their godly leaves
to speak in those distant voices just once more !

xcvi

the river at its crest takes night by the knees
drowns the effigies of sleep giving no warning
to daylight to the lesser denizens of the hours
highways wrapped around tree trunks and
the myth of horizons forever lost to the waters
so it goes the world on its spindle crazy to
fall this way or that and the skies and moss
all together in the dream of a budding flower
is there a way out ? does the path only go
to the end of the wood and then forever dark ?
who put us here to wander and wrestle with
rotted logs mulch swirling eddies a poetry
of exile and illness the shoulder to the wheel
and cities that come and go crystal fragments
fractions of number unuttered vowels a crash
in the somnolent ear the sodden consonants
that make up the dialed cipher the unspoken

ladder the statuettes lined up like cigarettes
in a silver box and the voice of unknown origins
that booms like an oracle separating twilight
from the hills it embroiders and tossed about
on a bed of reeds the shattered child the light
drawn from the bone and the cut two inches
in to the puzzled head however much it takes
to remember only to forget the following minute
whoever it was whatever mad design polyphonic
yet meaningless to find the way back is useless
the mountain of language the shadows of song
ancient and blind the lessons of the masters
protractions into the root and seed-bed and
finally exhaustion and weary the eye struggles
to understand the heaving outlines and forms
apparitions of a phantom world was never
here before did not recognize the sign smoke
the plural of air the very distances of echo
I am a thing drowned in the water of things
hand and lapse and a final breath release

xcvii

when four-fifths of the section is gone
and on the left the once perfectly hewn marble
gazing into its golden antiquity now stained
by acid time and the furlongs and paces
and widths by which we once determined
the distance to Pasargadae now as dust eddies
beneath tottering feet or knees that have
lost consciousness and sky once a thing
agape with swarms of azure empyreans
cloud flecked saddened dominion of missing
deities of imperfections and dilutions
that wrack the memory of a sea voyage

is it the Sirens in their rushing ambulance
of aesthetics and pornography who are diminishing
the number of days the routines dilapidated
in a siesta of troubling vowels and ciphers
of a unity once considered a philosophical
attribute but what is the concern when
waking to what might be a last hour
a porous minute of wasting and reflection
giving affection to those tones and hues
music and painting the aura of grief
that mantles the human shoulder a gravity
that is as impenetrable as the mountain
that overshadows us with the gift of
uncompromising sleep but the dream
between two mirrors and the face that sees
back to the child buried in the small disaster
of a glass with its dissolved orient breaking
on the cusp that divides silence from its
hemisphere of dappled oblivion the echo
of ink and the words in countless disorder
ink gives birth to an always unfinished poetry
like the futile struggle of rock formations
to become other than the remaining fifth
of the structure of breath and light

xcviii

the god whose domain is a grain of sand
and who lives for the instant only
who drives a rust colored automobile
down Figueroa Street in the year 1945
who has given us houses to exchange
furniture to embellish shadowy rooms
and grammar books and ornate peristyles
fountains and colored stones to toss

into pools smooth as jade and evenings
when the orange glow of a radio
emits songs of constant unending love
which is sorrow as well and ceilings
from which lanterns hang and fireflies
an age of dust and distance has given us
and to grieve that the moment has passed
when light eternal shone its haunted moon
overhead and we danced and murmured
unintelligible words to ears of stone
that god who has disordered the years
and made centuries come and go in a flicker
who dwells in the ruins of a drop of water
and destroys dawns in cataclysms of dew
whose name is inconstancy the unknown
has rendered us as statues smoking cigarettes
to wander lunatic across a separate inch
in search of the fiber that will color
echo with tempests of lost memory
has stolen sleep from rock and grass
has filtered vowels through aching leaves
has written with a swollen finger
immense tomes filled with mute consonants
that god invisible and bright as mercury
who takes the blame for every passing day
whose nerve and brain are refulgent
with the antipodes of space has won
the game of time and tossed us heedless
into the ditch where bone expels flame
a god such as this with his lotus reference
and eyes like swarming angry bees
his flashing glance and thunderous tongue
his dance at last the futile mountain top
where language excoriates its nonsense
to whom we pray and dream again

to whom we kneel unconscious the regained
wit the senseless litany of poems and thought
to create him was our grave error
to let him weave in and out of lives
to dispel hope and longing and renew
the cosmos in his single breath
all things are come to naught
in him whose mind is the shape of nothing
vast ink of unelaborated oblivion
tombstone of what never was

xcix

tengo ganas de morir
and yet does the green shoot
              in the light appear

all around are fire and accident
immobility of angels caught flying
stone in its effervescence to shift
into the immaterial world of hues and
shades of red incarnate in the *word*
tengo ganas de morir
moved by the chthonic deity of steps
into the upper realms and hosannas
and steeples of dizzying memory
on earth it was abuzz the freight of bees
aromas of dawn's sweet pantry
elegance of bone and flute playing
the erstwhile melody of time
tengo ganas de morir
awake for this brief instant ablaze
with all the fuse and fission of the eye
nerve and sinew of stammering tongue
alarms and bells dunning the ear
cliff and hill and residue of water

distances no more than an inch away
the heights of air and sleep
tengo ganas de morir
the leaf that shakes in its diameter
the math of sand and grit beneath the nail
fictions and prosody of the *vowel*
extinct before its enunciation !
mornings and more mornings
then grief the accent in its circumflex
sorrowing through rapturous syllables
tengo ganas de morir
no wonder the town exists no more
and coffins painted in their pride
go sliding into the fiery circle
a wheel a brace a remote desire
like quicksilver rising in its glass
to reach the highest element
in the curvature of things unknown
tengo ganas de morir
flowers that in their evening speak
while rock and grass yield to dew
intransigent the writing in the clouds
predictions of fray and defeat
lining and structure of the unconscious
as it parries its divided thrusts
into the dried wells of oblivion
tengo ganas de morir
and nothing less a printed flame
a shadow dancing on the wall
afternoons in school without recall
blackboard lozenge and spirals bright
come home to unclocked emptiness
raveling thought dense as echolalia
or moons repeated in an argent rill

tengo ganas de morir
and yet does the green shoot
               in the light appear

               c

in the shadow play of mortals
light is an accident in the conjecture of space
who plays the god and who dances with nymphs
who imitates the voice of the swan in flight
and who dies too young to remember
the shot-put that failed the toss of the dice
random proclivities among asterisks and comets
to be praised or damned and be cast
into the arroyo epithets of lost alphabets
with a consonant missing in the fierce and
mantic punctuation of the zodiac
to each a house is allotted and to error given
riding the simultaneous crest between
sleep and the dense dark wood
of wandering and grief and whosoever
emerges will not be of the same consciousness
but a stranger the other in a sequence
of disaster and approximation and from on high
if such a place exists the oracle trimmed
to a vocabulary of exactly seven vowels
resounds of stone and the graven image
polyglot references to sand and basalt
the pharaonic ear drilled with mysteries
like water pouring through a bipartite hand
it is to be human that the car brake ceases to work
or that the tide floods the mansion of dreams
it is to be quiet among the trees and to listen
the foliage ancient and dusky whispering
each leaf an archaic soul imprisoned

by the myth of language and doomed to repeat
one by one the disjointed syllables of its fate
winds take away the hills ocher and bare
the landscape of twilight settles in over
a world which is the opposite of distance
a place of pools that grieve and sorrow and where
an inch at a time memory is reconstructed
frail props of grass and dew and a remote bright
thought anchored to labyrinthine mind
birth and death in the instant of recovery
maze of things seen and heard in a previous life
unaccounted for and lost no sooner found
why is there a step not taken ?

ci

immortality resides outside the universe !
the entire cosmos is a Sanskrit prison-house
born and unborn seek release from the laws
of sun and moon and the horses that draw
them repeatedly from dawn to night and back
the dismembered human parts are the arcana
of distance light and space and the stars
without number but the aggregate of gods
multiple without origin unpronounced *sounds* !
ephemera phenomena enigma and *Breath*
meet me tomorrow at the ice-cream parlor
and I'll explain the rest to you just loan me
your hair your cranium your left knee
the nerves and sinew that govern your mind
trifling ideas in a spoon plate glass reflections
of an afternoon that exists outside of time
you and me us and them the whole tripartite
division of earth and sky and what lies in between
and do you remember the time coming home

from the movies and we played dead in the park
how long it took us to die and to be reborn
the soul is merely a reflexive pronoun
hidden etymologies and texts of homophones
litanies of vowels darkening at the root before
the great phonetic explosion of before and after
to put it another way as we rose dusting ourselves off
blades of grass half-intuitions of the other side
where who we are is not who we were coming
and going through husks of lexicons a breath
divided by five and the droning chant of stone
filling the ear with silences that occur between lives
a leaf an oracle a diapason water rushing
in its blind lunar passion to become empty !
are we identity or only the resemblance to identity ?
it takes years to wake up but less than an instant
to realize and forget that we are connected
are we at the top or the bottom of understanding ?
a bird trill a rain-drop a sequence of lightning
buried in rock nothing but echoes of echoes
the two of us running then not running stock still
to listen to the noise sleep makes entering the wind
it is for us to remain asleep not remembering
hearing but not hearing the seed increasing
its terrific vital force non-dual and undefined
one of us will be at the other end waiting

cii
++++++++++++++++++++++++++++++++
houses built like matchboxes slanted
on the western hill where one evening you
will arrive confused as to which is yours
din of kitchen ware and scullery oaths
oils seeping between consonants of fear

which god will lay sheet over golden sheet
and bathe dress and perfume your consort
the fish-eyed goddess of cave and depths
prepared to shine on the rocky imminence
language weighed on the scales of lunation
fusion of sound to gravity as mind empties
by daybreak when seas of distance glitter
when the opaque black sun of recrimination
sets its compass toward evolution zero
suddenly eternal night snatches at your ankles
raveling dusky ropes up to your knees
to topple you head first into the sea-board
where the startled noon of statues blazes
whatever indistinct last vowels you will hear
or the creaking wain with its stone wheels
and stumbling oxen faint and trembling
++++++++++++++++++++++++++++++++++++
what is formidable and the lack of justice and
on high an indistinct sun pandering to the god
of lost directions the illustrated matter at the end
of the book and the constant and grieving felt
each time the soul wakens to the tune of fireflies
yet there is no other thing in sight and mind
stirs on its ancient porch asking the subtleties
to be redefined and the heavens in a swirl
of skirts and ironed collars bleach and lavender
will the most archaic of thoughts come circling
round to the faded orient that gave it birth ?
come home to the residues of matter imploring
memory to become static a purpose in rock
a thrill hidden among the cloying grasses
underfoot where Proserpina danced of a moonlit
hour and the trees in their polyglot whisperings
spent leaf after leaf in the Spain of light
no more is there a hand to hold nor a mouth

bereaved to seal and listen for the dark waves
a beauty in the depthless waters a reflection
that you once were enamored in the fan of senses
drawing a comb through untamed hair like
asterisks dense and wild in the starless night
++++++++++++++++++++++++++++++++++++++
face down in the bed of sounds
ear at the root where sirens drown

ciii

there was no next day no reason to shave
the corpse in its entirety the cosmos itself
floating vague as a soap bubble into thin air
cloud and warp and masonry of thought
evaporated among the planetary ruins
often unseen drifting from the sprockets
of memory the hour to the minute the ghost
captured momentarily then released from
the photographic plate and ascending silvery
from the bottom up wafting sheets aloft
swirling invisible patterns used to be breath
a small wasted conjunction between two great
luminous paragraphs you might say a russet
colored gown fit over the head or a shroud
rather and the face the features of a statue
a stuttering effigy you might call it with
some renown was evidence of walking on earth
each hand a flutter like bird's wings high and
soft almost boneless the history of a republic
never born simply on the coast with its cities
nascent articles to be employed in case of speech
each carefully placed rock each stone endowed
with magic or a sun blacker than expected alone
in its porphyry sky you might mistake it for

a form of religion fire-worshipping altars
bluish smoke intaglios beautiful and wispy
rising into the paradise of copy-boys and mice
Apollo fragrant with hyssop and day-old wine
taking them into his embrace and weeping for
some mysterious reason the oracular apse the dome
around him about to collapse and the obsidian
features traced on the moving wall behind him
myth and sadness accompanying the shifts
each vowel just once before gone the enigmatic
interstices where perception turns to hieroglyph
will we never come back to that secret place
where we first learned then so swiftly forgot
what it was ?

civ

if there is a god in stone and another one
in the air we breathe and three more in each of
the places we set markers to direct the wind
and fiercely wanton several more rising out
of sea-foam and mountain crest and delivered
by sleep into thoughtlessness a great one for dreams
if there are so many and multiple gods too with
heads of crocodile or dog or serpent and polyglot
and issuing from crevice of earth and sulfur
who govern not only stairways but the tops
and bottoms of the entries to the various
levels of the under-earth and of trees and their
thousands of countless leaves that have a secret
language and of children who dwell in a maze
of kite-string and ebullition of unknown holidays
even more gods some lachrymose others painted
like naked rosy buttocked cherubim and some who
only appear in plate glass windows holding Chinese

fans who recite drunken poetry and bridges falling
slipped from the divine hands of the maker of waters
and especially of love and its unfortunate deviations
gods tantalizing of aspect profoundly beautiful as ruins
marble sleek lying scattered across the fields of heaven
feet of gods fern and moss talking plenty and huge
in the aerial dimensions of hope and progress but none
so distant and enviable as the one who dominates
life the give and take of mask and ego gown and shift
adornments of shining and decay the other side of
light and suns blacker than pitch moving through
the quadrants that design disaster and mortal
spans the never sure of understanding the pivoted
into excess of zeal and wounded by passion who
inhabit the *you* and *I* in our steeple chase around
the enormous vacated cities of the eighteenth century
what is to give to reason ? what is to subtract
from illumination ? gods of chicanery and deceit
who are not concerned with justice who play
with foil and rapier and in a trice snatch breath
from the least likely of our children and laugh on
balconies of gas and tin the ever remote gods
the founders of cosmic disorder and event horizons
absent from the ever dissolving vowels of meaning
abstract lunatics each a god for every thought that
has disrobed the quintessence of being human
gods and more who revolve in dust motes
shaking the glass of reverie and of death especially
white robed haunting phantom gods hieroglyphs
of the broken promise of immortality

if there is a god in stone

cv

who will be saved and are there not
cloisters enough the tread of earth worn bare
and ascending almost invisible the soul
like a crystal in fourteen shades burning
in the noon of the eye what is most beyond
outline of the mountain and the heights
purplish with heather running skirts folded
toward the sea bank where mermaids lie
drying the tangled masses of their hair
and is not salvation a concept only a notch
on the thought that wakes and dies forlorn
etched like carbon against the passing wall
will you then or I meet again in these corridors
to discuss what mind implores in aggravation
of a last day in time or the swelter of compound
consonants in their forest southern with oozing
resin and the pitch and odor of tanneries climbing
up from the cities now abandoned in their shells
will not others too strive for redemption
illustrating the waning hour with ciphers
of mystical purport the sun's raft riding high
amongst the vowels and cinders of deep regret
a sea there is up there where elevators cannot go
and waves of sleep and machines that drone
like hives of vedic mantras and there in stone resolved
the head weighs its consequences and runs
a vision beatific all shimmering the white
of the afterlife reconsidered the gravid accent
the circumflex and asterisk the leveled noun
until remains in all perplexity a man's only life
two days here a week there submerged in phosphorous
and doors and stairs and wells where urns
are filled with endless water and the season
of bird and serpent and the dragon's tail

soughing among the embittered leaves
how many tales left untold the sins of youth
redrawn on the empty canvas a reddened sign
a hand still weaving its counterpart and the mouth
left to breathe its final rosary a lingering
such as few words can bring to the soul's brief
a wing aflutter smoke from a candle gone out

cvi

red dawn crescent over the flown sands
flung far from the Sanskrit mountain
midden heap of history trolls and fawns
pawning over detritus of temple relics
fire altars grown cold in siege of letters
none so profound as the grief-graven stele
half of which governs noon the other half
lost in the puerperal mists where writing
has no force serves no purpose but where
wanes love's image the shape and swell
of philosophy wave and weave spell the air
darkening as the signs drained lose sense
of night and the constellations of ruddy
afterthought pilgrimage of stars and moon
a waist a crupper an amber hair-comb
visions of a goddess fleet of foot naked in mind
only across suburban fields where spotted deer
still lick salt blocks and the reading of a text
more ancient than ink drones into the Hour
smaller punctuation the waves that lap at her
skirts and the red-eyed hound chasing her shadow
the delicate reverie soon it will be the day before
yesterday the almanac open to the last season
fall of leaves turned by the planet mercury
into language and messages from the dead

x-ray ambulance and foot-guards at the portal
above the lone hawk unhooded shrieks a cry
heart rending where is the mystery fled ?
painted memories fade and pale on ruined walls
a river between the gesso hills to the west
iron and blaze of unfinished war-epic and
the asterisk of reunion between breaths
lapsed into the golden hiatus of Pythagoras
so many cities gone from the vanished horizon
loud symptoms in the ear dwelling in grass
stone effigies pointing puzzled toward a sky
hanging like a tropical canopy over sleep
all hazy the terminal thoughts the elusive
phantom speech acts and ineffable silence

where is the mystery fled ?

cvii

how far does sky go and where does it begin
and where does it end or is it only the hieroglyph
worn in the hair-piece of goddess Isis ?
thirteen years since I last saw my twin effigy
middle of a naked summer with its eternity
of sky and concrete and the hullabaloo of
divinity and the quality of mortal life
a butterfly the soul of my lost son gone into
the flues and traits of a post-modern infinity
charged with mercury and light to ascend forever
into sky the everlasting intemporal intangible
there is no puzzle or labyrinth more enigmatic
than sky the boundless unincorporated space
in the wink of an eye that comes and goes
like a blade of grass burdened by a dew-drop
or the flight of a moth blinded by the flame
of desire the heights where the other half goes

to curl up and die and the endless solemnity
of the corpse on its drifting barge to reckon
with the darkened sun of the after-world
and hail once and for all the goddess in her
raiment of farewell and grief charged with bright
punctuation sequins of precious stones and sand
the isolated instant when she dissolves into sky
and returns the next minute bearing sky
on her lap to suckle though with sorrow filled
her generous breast and all that history ignores
the initiation and the last rites in one ecstatic
moment orgasm of thunder and waterfall
pitch of the oriental note and riverrun hues
sky in all its ephemeral shining a hymn
to distance and to what can never return
and yet there we are forever on our backs
on an atavistic lawn in the middle of an epic
not hearing the saws and spears of battle
staring hypnotized into the traveling sky
with its vowels of lost aviators and angels
future come and gone the minute we lay there
chrysalis of azure in which a child is born
only to die of his own surfeit of wing and flight
where sky cannot begin where sky can never end
possessed by the butterfly and its divinity
as brief as human life sky infinitely blue

cviii

borne forth from the light as is gold
from dross and night what spirits dwell
invisibly in the breath released and
forces innate the animal in its lair
closed to the inner eye and where upper
stairs lead to the path narrow as a finger

singing is great and hymns to Cythera
for as some say poetry is love and what
of the histories and their impounded
values and livestock and the mountain
that abounds in fractured syllables
darkness which is malleable as air
in its enormous winnowing cycles
to have arrived on earth and walked
among such statues blind relics of an hour
when speech and leaves were one and
wind the trajectory of animus and anima
tempests in the candle's brief flame
and to have known yet never understood
cave and height wherever the path
in its anguish led and there inside the myth
nymph and hair and pool and shimmer
how was one ever to get memory back ?
glint of sulfur in the glowering clouds
loom and restoration of an archaic text
words bottomed out for meaning vowels
like shapes of sleep dancing in the hills
who will ever comprehend this was life ?
a hand a mistake a sketch of beauty
in inks of unfathomable hues and
to sleep it all away from day One
and the zero of apotheosis and rock
above and below the glade a mystery
where Persephone misstepped the sudden
crevice yawning below her feet pitch
and bitumen the reek of tanneries
in the Maghreb solitary recollection
by which the mind wakes to dawn
enigmas stretching out like deserts
what flower will ever bloom so white
and red alike as the stain on her cheek ?

aulic stanzas forged and numinous
dissolving in an oracular mist
a single space or many ?

cix

not in excess of twenty years more and set
the futile anvil to its bed a host of phantoms
scouring the eastern sky and thunder too
green and irrevocable will you know it ?
adorn a rock and expect advice from it
in the tiny hollow of a henna tinted palm
a goddess *the* goddess to arise fully painted
upper lip more swollen than the lower
heaven the flash of lightning in her eyes
Bedouins and the like genuflecting in dust
hand-me-downs of history shattered or
spent in the restless inch devouring time
what have you learned from this book-learning
but the oaths and recriminations of ego ?
spoils and taunts the iridescent night a fever
frames sleep in its ivy-curled intaglio
depths that cut either way through winds
asked from which island did you sail and
what are you seeking on this tedious voyage
outward into waters hitherto unknown
the great and yawning abyss of sky tumult
and roar of concave and opaque distances
nor will you find rest but in a whirligig
of hours and unconsciousness will descend
to the house of mysteries unkenned sapped
of virtue and defense hands quivering with ague
feet slipping in the morass of memories
leaf and raiment torn and sullied harvest
of moons that have gone underground

what will you answer ? tangled in sheets
dreaming the goddess of lamps will embrace
you giving you strength to move again even
if among shadows and nameless phantoms
who have been trained to run machines
awed by the mere recollection of that realm
stuttering what kind of answer can you give ?
grieving it was beside the vacant temple
listening for the vowels locked in marble
looking ever askance at the body of stars
raining down on the unattainable horizon
either you will shift into the dusky hills
a mass of organized cellular activity
weeping for the ones who became absent
in that meaningless labyrinth of light
or you will cease to partake of the air
suffused with sulfurous beams eddying
around your ivy-girt temples a statue
given to human tears and puzzlement

stone at one end of paradise stone at the other

cx

the repetitious round of the days
as they come and go circling the invisible
whole the diameter without purpose
the sound of echo patterned after echo
the sum of memory the Monday equidistant
from Monday and all that occurs in between
the line drawn from the sun's molten center
to the trace on earth where Dionysus
is celebrated for keeping the vine intact
for nurturing seed and leaf alike and
yet the always and yet of human frailty
of the division between breath and light

and the finite distance of the eye small
in its nerve-mass reflecting mirage of
the outside world where the soul hovers
burdened by the body within palpitating course
of red and white corpuscles and history
renewed and destroyed in every pulse beat
the greater alliances of thought and space !
which god deceives us about these matters ?
the trifling of x-ray and mineral deposit
the child within the man the woman who is both
indivisible and ascendant superior to the realm
of almanac and month and who inspires
breathing deep into the rock fragments
that compose the mental being the grammatical
self the vowel and tortured consonant of
the encrypted mind in its quire of alphabets
days to come are the days that have already been
multiple egos of a single imagination !
the wheel and loom of the stars constantly
churning and minting the illustration
that gives to each minute its own death to each hour
the breath to revive until the last spoke
has been turned and there is no more language
to describe the vast nullity of events
lost in the labyrinth and similitude of days
remote instant at the beginning
and end of infinity

cxi

diaphanous plurality of space
in the wink of an eye turns to darkness
singular and without history other than
the consciousness that has imagined it
grain and structure of myth in rock crystal

emerging shadows figures of speech come to light
misrepresentations of life the coil unwinding
bent over the corpse to exhume hope
tragedy in its five acts curtain and sash
the rapier flashing in the corners and a cloak
damaged goods the elements of nature
matter at its worst docked for its imperfections
come to the shores pre-dawn to watch the breakers
sullen waves rushing to take the names out to sea
tide and vowel of the oracular moment
who will give back to mortals their memory ?
wasteland and empire both lost in chronicles
jeopardy and illumination leaping from mountain
to mountain in the first hours of creation
the generations of men flipping rapidly like pages
of an unwritten book paragraphs of mutilated
passion and envy and the desire to ascend
to sublime heights the poesy of inspiration
and madness fictions of language or aphasia
music replete with unheard notes floods the ear
like the time in the used car lot when angel
fell to earth rust and oil slicks and a drain pipe
amazement and instantaneous brilliance
like a shower of stars at midday dazed and
disoriented angel was put on a stretcher and taken
to the nearest emergency room for x-rays
and a drug that would make him forget everything
such is the peculiar and only moment of insight
we strike from order the chance for disorder !
looking to the heavens clouds gathering dialects
gods half-drunk imitating themselves !
so many speech acts witless despair of the moment
who was born to die first who was left to mourn
enacted on the screen flickering and argent
the grey black forms shifting across the retina

not for me ! cries an off-stage voice
it is beyond the polyvalent air that surrounds
mind perpetuating itself in false recognitions

Buddha Shiva Jesus !
drop-box of compassion and loss
diaphanous plurality of space

cxii

white feet as dust grazing shadows
Artemis her fantasy to delve into light
entwined with gossamer of memory her thoughts
to bring as a lamp to disorder the bright seed
and scatter with deft hand into the fosse
there will grow flowering the spring hues
sea the color of granite and sky rushing
to take into its skirts the Sicilian fields
lush with the circular heat of the underworld
soon is never too late to chase the stag
and vie with her brother keen Apollo the dart
aims so straight and evening finds death
around her ankles in soft blue petals

cxiii

to be burnt and cast to the winds sacred wood
the cloister and marble of memory shed
its luster time itself the dross clinging to night
in shreds of lamp-sphere and whatever else
jasper or emerald and the twinkling
of sea-gaze in moonlight wave over wave
rushing to eat the shore where ghosts walk
spear in hand helmet in search of a head
cognition of things perishes in fine salt breeze
the ends as a man the frivolous afternoons
wasted in the false eden of a drugstore

perfumes chocolates glass darkly shining
back against a reflection of the world as a stain
who roam errant lost without true north
voices unraveling in a pink-frilled shell
where sleep embeds its dead troubadours
with lute and dim song strings untuned
the many hours spent in the grammar of dusk
hills running to be consecrated and *Gong !*
thunder in the sky's darkening veins green
in depth like the inches of moss and fern underfoot
holy altars abandoned in tangle of mad ivy
shrine to the goddess of the well turned ankles
of the hemline rimmed with white dust
leaving no footprint elevated as a single thought
in the chrysalis of air hovering above rock
where has the sun gone to these days ?
for upwards of five thousand years love's
effigy more and more indistinct a hieroglyph
carved in basalt and the tongues of satyrs
of beings without name of leering gargoyles
whatever the underworld has borne to destroy
these earths of multiple mirrors and pond scum
when was there ever an Arcadia but this
selva oscura dread cypress growing dense
by irregular arroyos a thin gilt to the transept
beyond which the planet ebbs dizzyingly
is one to put the ear to the cliff-hedge
to listen for the echo ? mind is a haze !
fragments mere fragments crumbling
the finger as it turns lost forever
in the vagrant etymology of grass

cxiv

whatever else I have said or done
to wonder at the reverie of words
a husk I am and ever shall be in winds
driven by dark torment and smaller light
a thread woven in unwritten space
dim spool spinning around a single memory
stone and verger and copse grown wild
by the fallen gate and profound abyss
when was to dance ? what was the score ?
sleeps still the Madonna of the wood
undone her braid put to rest her mind
sun for her is less bright this noon
and the parade of flute and brass that trills
the events that will never come to pass
what of this hour a hedge of diminishment
cannot return to that unlit room nor
by the charge of a dampened flare read
the writing in the folds of grass
this it is a history of tarnished golds
of edgeless silver in moons and fireflies
of porches where echoes of pale girls
whose faces immersed in budding blooms
are now forgotten as ash or cinder block
that holds shut the cavern's door
I cannot say which day it is nor its hue
and tense nor what space it occupies
however brief the instant of it may be
a disappearance like all the others behind
walls of mutant moss and shale or
ivy twined around the wasp-thin waist
of *She* whose job it is to put the candle out
pronouns of wax and wane we are
blind and deaf insects burrowing in dung
wingless images that yearn to fly

amidst this nameless swarm I wend
tripping from rock to rock a cloud
a wen a mere dew-drop derelict
in the forest and maze of mind
asleep as ever dreaming that I was once
a father and a child a brother too
a tombstone tossed to the waves
a mist ascending an alphabet of air
fickle ending to a rosary of words
trailing into oblivion's eternity

cxv

fandangos of dust the ancient !
my heart in the middle of the deepest lake
and sizes of ink so great the sky flounders
inching toward its own sleep
castles of a water that reaches its arm
into the haunted mountain and Spanish
caballeros riding backwards on a fleet
sad-eyed the Madonna of under-things
wearing rings of human bone
bracelets necklaces and charms that sing
hair three miles long and wilder
than the blackest thought of man
her mind is a pyramid and in her eyes
the moon fires salvos of ruddy doubt
bringing down the seas of antiquity
at the bottom of the deepest lake
where I lay dreaming with my *zopilote*
cities of leopard skin and parchment
go weaving through waves of silken haze
what is to drown in such superfluity ?
I gain an inch on my scabbard
and ply each summer storm with thrusts

of cloud and nacre and build to the top
a tree of sacred mineral by threes and fours
children agape at the crystal rise
shout with glee their fundamental toy
thunder and its enemies strive
to win and chastise *Nuestra Señora* la Sierra Madre
whose serpents are doubled in her skirts
dancing madly she swallows the Sanskrit vowel
turning the universe into an eye of flame
witless conquistadors go tumbling
with their ire for gold and plunge
each a feather into the pyre
never was a dumbness so secure
and knots that gnarl in the throat
Corazón ! the way is always in and out
but never all the way around and
thick miles of ash and leafy mulch
where drown the words that cannot save
she dances madly on her consonant of skull
her syllables tripartite that ring like brass
in the shattered ear of stone
a girl a firefly a drug that makes you *see*
she leads the way through labyrinth
and maze a furl and circumflex
that crowns the undivided sound
alone I am with her at last
in the graveyard of infinity

cxvi

closed the small circle and found peace
indivisible silence of the after-time
the hour when all ceases to have weight
when gravity and matter are reconciled
the minute-hand fused to its lost space

the leaf against the pane grown dark
and the lamp withdrawn in its replica
shines no more inside the shattered will
in Brooklyn by the Gowanus Canal where
no insect dares to dwell the world found
its beginning in an x-ray of the end
from as far as Rockaway bird shrills
call in the cloudless no-where heavens
transistor radios held to the sidewalk
"Do the Hustle" whispered in the ear
how could so much vitality be condensed
in an instant that took 40 years to fulfill ?
in the basements of dry-goods stores
or where Xmas trees hang upside down
a phantom child flickers here and there
a magic wand and eyes like swift fireflies
feet that skip and hop a small fandango
down the fast and vanishing thoroughfares
shadowless in an ambulance he disappears
no warning for the disease he bore
just the ticker-tape of machines recording
the heart's ennui and breath's despair
bringing night to its endless conclusion
a soul flown from earth's flowering inch

closed the small circle and found peace

cxvii
the death that lives in all of us
to indulge in specious post-modernist
arguments about Sanskrit poetics or to
rail against the petty invective of Horace
ignoring the unities of wave and shore
salt boundaries that become indivisible
with light and the great atmosphere that

surrounds organic activity and rock
opera resounding between cliff and storm
heights of imponderable suns dizzying
splendors of sea-bottoms scalloped shells
mermaids of impossible hair-masses and
the Apollonian music of lyre and vowel
sanctifying irretrievable meters of echo
long submerged in the stoned ear of dreams
bard and muse fission and implosion of
et cetera granite silver topaz omicron
destruction of Troy ten times over and
numeration of corpses piled on each other
legend of skin blanched by a frosted moon
hands that never touch and grasses torn
blade by blade from memory of earth
alive no more ! yet lapsed into the deep pool
of mind invertebrate skeleton of thought
lingering deposit of sound clinging to marble
fragments everything hashed and ripped
brain's eerie and errant shadow haunting
bed and tomb fuses and petals and ears
to bring everything together forgetting
literature and its wasteland afternoons
on drowsy Capri drunk on wines of eternity
when did language come into being and
why do imprecision and imperfection reign ?
search the underside of glass retract each
syllable of the Osiris-text and scatter
bone and sand the lists of all the kings
dash to the ground the broken femur
reading with alert thumbs the ogive and
acanthus and rave into the Buddha's cave
the single and transparent consonant
nothing can ever be pronounced aright
sleepers in the woof of space depart !

footnotes commas ampersands unlit
regions of the farflung orient a planet
in search of its crematorium anklets ringing
in foreboding of the final hour feminine
in its grammatical context and opaque !
how far back the mystery reaches
unscripted losses and sorrow
the grieving leaves the soft

the death that lives in all of us

cxviii

enough to say the ending has happened
multiple times a version on the screen
followed by real-life swings to sick bays
and the paraphernalia of breath and ticking
registers that underline in red the heights
of Mercury the darker realms of Pluto
passageways that lead nowhere but under
and the haunting array of broken mirrors
where Persephone tries to reconstruct her face
gemmed aureoles turning dark in morbid
breezes no thirst slaked and Sirens ululating
inaudible decibels at a frequency no ear
can withstand have been here twice before
it seems a human without memory gazing
on his own ruin marble fractured at the waist
bent looking for the pool that has stolen
his reflection and what doesn't bear weight
only lists to the side of a threatened water
bark and rent sail tattered by the wind
is it to go further south to reckon with the dead
or is it only to stand there shaking both hands
multiplied by a desire simply to hold
what is behind the sudden wall opaque

and riddled with a quizzical ivy strangling
fundament and air-hole alike the Roman
category of mystery painted in ruddy hues
on the failing stucco distance how does it
adhere to the mind already a disarray of
thought and mirage absent of recollections
grass patches sinking turf marsh and bog
in the midst of which Queen-of-the-Night
displays her eerie white petals not far from
the real ending the final punctuation damp
enigma of root and eyeless worm sorrowing
pronouns lacking the structure of vowel
and accent am I alone with such a wreckage
asylum given to no one slipping from the path
into the bedrock of alienation and ennui
severed already from the love that bore me
to this terminus where the god of smoke and
stairways lays his snares reciting sotto voce
as ever the basement and the cup and horse

lost noons !

cix

five in the morning *Bong!* iridescent
the enormous vowel that escapes thought
beverage of clouds passing through the moon
stellar hiatus in the sea of tranquility
buried in stone memory and its other *echo*
nothing born from nothing and life
born from *sound* the undeliverable instant
when burning the cosmos rewinds itself
five in the morning *Bong!* nostalgia of fireflies
swarming from the indelible consonant
which is both light and the promise of light
the rising sun blacker than yesterday

hieroglyph of impotent deities clinging
to the sand of their unformed destinies
what is there to build and destroy again ?
cities of grass and marble wavering in dew
five in the morning *Bong!* fluorescent
as the vast cavities of hospitals and dust
mountain defiles and phalanxes of hoplites
prepared to defend the liberty of rock !
at no hour in time is solitude greater
than this illusory slipping from mind
into depths of hyacinth and jade immortality
in vain the mirror is scoured for contours
of the missing face the envelope of hair
aphasic edges of an unuttered word
five in the morning *Bong!* inspiration to
overcome the window and its projections
toward either hemisphere of sleep
night's infirmity riddled with falling stars
a continent of gas extending nebulae
into the still point of the soul where weights
and measures are of no consequence
only the small and unlit punctuation
marking the limit to human possibility
five in the morning *Bong!* the ineffable
++++++++++++++++++++++++++++++++
whirring of wings a leaf
between darkness
and darkness

cxx

my broken heart

Max was in the churning of the ocean
when Vishnu's throat turned blue
was in the spit of land yearning to touch

salt where eternity begins its march
was in the alphabet of errors spilling
from the comet's wasted tail the ruptured
light of ragged lamps that line the corridors
where doctors fail to explain just why
was in the vacuum tube and spark plug and
incandescent hand that flicks the switch
that turns on and off the elevator that never stops
was in the omicron and hyacinth and vowel
that divides hour from hour the wall
and stairs and doors that cannot read
in the outside of instamatic reconditioning
in the equidistant corners of unknown space
where x-rays propel a distance of pure ink
in the desk tops and laboratory valves
in the men in white who are illegible and
in the nurses dressed in frocks of limitation
Max was on the boat that sank in ether
on its voyage to the west of ten
his strength was in the unwinding finger
pointing to the invisible Friend
to the stranger at the lintel with his soaps
and dented lace the cosmic personification
of a pronoun that has no use Max
was in the clarinet Mozart employed just once
in the cabaret of notes that define bedlam
and the mind's vain attempts at speech
Max was in the statue by the pond of depths
the marble of ventriloquism the radiophonic
memory that imitates the echo of red wires
in the sleeping grass below the roof
and in the animals and tree trunks
that play hide and seek with afternoons
in the siren an ambulance makes becoming destiny
or in the infinite explosion of writing when

it inscribes a small dot to mark the end of time
in the least of us he persists
unnumbered leaf a rhyme of air and dew
and darkest night the bed of all

cxxi

in birth the second after is the first of death
linger long as you want over the deep water
or stop to fix the mirror's errant code
the flowers that bind their hues to vast night
are there no more to touch their petals
fallen into some miasmic snow or torn
from the syllables they represented of a day
is it to speak of love and forensic decay
to wander over hills of ocher drafts and spines
the circle of trees in their conspiracy to withhold
messages of light or the houses blackened
by the small tumult of an absence no one recalls
and which is the way and the road gone wrong
the frail anemones and their planted beds
the hour you least expect is the one
when all time halts and the noise outside
and the recitation of the bard in his steep drink
glorious and varied the epic lines about seas
and islands that cannot be and
the multitude of names mispronounced and
tossed into the rusting can the heroes you imagine
to have warped their shields leaping over walls
to bring down a city with its hundred haunted women
tarrying back and forth over nocturnal walks
all this is no more than a sleight of hand
a murmur in the ear of one about to die
and though just born and bright and playing
in grasses no longer than a summer and

from on high comes the missile that strikes
and flings the head from life to stone
inscriptions illegible incisions on stained marble
funerary urns and deposits of ash and rust
the entire history of the western ecumene
half-buried in a temple ruin tilted against
a mountain filled with unknown vowels
and sounds that only occur in dreams and yes
the birthday you thought would come around
the famous day with its tins and trumpets
is just an asterisk at the bottom of a page
squiggles and spills of an eternal ink
meant to spell out a clear destiny
fictions ! birth and death the talking leaf
whispering just once *the end is here*

cxxii

a flimsy orange wheelchair and
a skeleton of breath lingering
in a deconstructed memory of earth
street names that have been reversed
the end that all have seen on a bench
noon reveries in an enclosed park
heat draws its skirts in great red circles
and sun blackens in his fierce tower
while unseen rowers ply splintered oars
across a mythic Ionian water and cries
of gull and kestrels of forlorn wings
high in the empyrean's raging cliffs
which corner to turn which warp to weave
garages of silence lay their oils down
and shattered glass reflects history's
misery the untold efforts not just
to survive but to revive the body's soul

hoisted banners flapping among words
waiting to be released the utter chance
that another day will bring relief
shapes of sleepers rising from strange beds
who have yet to wake and light a lamp
and hold something like a flower
in hands only fever knows the ague
and pitch of a labyrinthine dream
nothing sorted out but combs and jibs
suitcases packed and whistles and smoke
the long voyage to an unplanned orient
gurus bonzes seers and palm-readers
Egyptian speech acts revolved in sands
summer after summer in a single hieroglyph
and awnings where catastrophes wait
to take back the empty cities of Troy
where to place the trembling foot
to reunite shadow with its traveling other
rename the ancient skies ! thirteen death
the foreign building where darkness
assumes its galaxy in the vowel
that yearns to be pronounced like July
the last was all the hour we needed
to say forever and farewell

cxxiii

horizon without horizons
planet of empty numbers
mind devoid of thought !
what else but a brow lit
by fireflies of unreason
profoundly soundless echoes
edges of an unspoken vowel
consonant of absent moons

all the in between gestures
that make sky uninhabitable
but for lost angels and seraphim
the captured isosceles triangle
the inverted pyramid of rust
leaves agitated by invention
of speech and corrupted memories
of days when arithmetic was
unknown artifacts of hand
and eye measurements of
distance and emptiness
when finally the gods
in their unruly palaces
ungovernable horses statues
kinetic and destructible amok
ruled the empyrean
giving birth to hapless mortals
giving death to the uncounted
the broken spark the unhinged
portal at the entrance
to the necropolis of poetry
line after line of blank syllables
voices without function
identities in search of an afternoon
masks and head-gear caskets
wrappings shrouds two o'clock !
Juno Mercury and Pluto
descant and declension
or merely the wind
dissolving light
whispers of
eternity

cxxiv
thirteen death

what day this is I don't know
what summer in time if there is one
july it's all a jumble is Joe back yet
he's in the next room when will he
wake up just a minute ago what hour
is it in this suffocating heat lying
there next to him blue wasps at
the window enormous predicates or
another premonition am I dead or
just born the water tower on the hill
the terraced slope of months briefer
than yesterday's kerchief a muffled cry
the mistake of language of knowing
if it is the right word the correct pronoun
the honorific moon-rise the stabilized
vowel in the midst of this roiling tempest
is Joe back yet he left his maps here
I cannot figure out if it's today already
I have grown up become a man learned
to do all kinds of unimportant things
the wisdom to just stop not open another
book there now easy around the corner
I can catch a glimpse of him he's
crying something about departures
and the large red hospital yesterday
in the garage with the lawn-mower
and being secretive hiding something
from me a direction or an alloy that
has magical powers and I can see around
the lilac hedge or where the hollyhocks
lift their necks craving more sun
today just keeps going in circles into
a concrete wall a sidewalk with graffiti

a totem beast lurking behind the tree
and trees have atmosphere & spirituality
not like museums and the leaves alert
to the nuances of speech and memory
I know it's almost there and the highway-
sound distant menace of soaring bees
shaking the air with a dense rumor
of death and the movie was in Joe's face
the one we loved to watch like mountains
gliding through clouds of sulfuric embrace
gods quarantined for their love affairs
heroes drawn from the quivers of night
shot through with amphetamines and turpentine
the deaths of the many in their automobile
mouths stuffed with grass and song
is it already the other time displaced
from the sign and its incredulous tome
am I still in a daze counting buildings
as they fall into silent waters and is it
still that afternoon heat in rising spires
and wheels and budgets of misbelief
stoned sequences of Mayan pre-history
wearing sandals and feathers in Teotihuacan
a hundred summers in a knuckle-bone
minutes without repair a shirt drenched
in ivy sweat and the price of heaven's
collateral and so much I cannot recall
is Joe still asleep in the other room ?

cxxv

the body made its own decision assigning
itself enough ink to last seven hours
then the *Gong!* and other futile alarms went off
could not understand what was going on

shutting shop closing the back door
cancelling airline flights and the one railroad
coach that goes due west and beyond the puny
range of pinnacles encumbrances slowly being shed
no more need to sweat to drain blood the wrong way
to drench the sheets in a yellow stain
life was already a lack of definition a Wednesday
without further setbacks an oval or a hiatus
a punctuation in the middle of nowhere
sequence of vowels and bodhisattvas lined up
in the corridor becoming invisible phantom
translations of an unwired medical cognition
sublimity in the form of a cloud or a cranium
memory no more distance without horizons
loud artifact of silence ! hands rumored to change
shape and identity and wherever the eye turned
ether and the massive history of stone
dense inevitability which is loss of gravity
its own decision heedless of the name's ego
the child inside the child multilayered wistful
riddled eternity of the instant it all disappears
magic maps of nowhere and silhouettes
transparencies glowing door-knobs footfalls
where flowers grew vast nebulae spiral out reaching
for a grammar of oblivion the release of tension
the body loosed of its freight undesignated
gone the underpinnings and hopes simply
the unfelt and enormous dissolution of matter
a poetry of vanishing dots and unreal ciphers
nothing and less than nothing the all
and the none which is space before
and after the explosion of light

cxxvi
the twins return to mexico

white shadow of rock in the afternoon's blank
hour the vestige of leaf the whispering echo
of talk in the small ink cast by the wall
painted emblems in the wind taking up its
skirts and the sudden blast of cloud tremor
the epic instant of delivery and recuperation
of the senses realizing without knowing it
that eternity has come and gone before the eye
seeing blindly the terrific suspense of light
curtains of disorganized matter and swarming
the zoom of bee and intellect and we swoon
in that unsound sleep of stucco drift
beside one another lambent and unseen waves
like ichor of the gods flowing freely through
our veins and a mythopoeic murmur of old
rustles in the ear's labyrinthine memory
time has stilled its fall in a heat of integers
pyramids to climb ! songs to unearth !
we travel within and without the great dust
beloved of dead angels and highwaymen
wearing our pluperfect shirts of mayan zigazag
we move south on the *carretera panamericana*
toward a hustle of Aztec meat market and blood
weaving through a single destiny shared by
the detritus of the mountain's history a column
aspiring to be a cathedral in the Zócalo
shivers on the elaborate skin of our oblivion
back and forth between the fireflies of music
dancing in a reverie with a thousand and one
simultaneous girls before the monsoon
this single instant is it all of 1953 ?
art and its planets we have come to worship
a knee on the revolving moving-picture that

spins around the phantom beds of desire and death
look high ! hospitals of water and gold
surfaces increasing the volume of sky with alcohol
roads and powders and magic vowels
repeated until space is reduced to a single unit
a peyote bud a rooftop and a quagmire
to run amok and yet stand shock still a numeral
in the frenetic jazz of the unheard note !

you and me Bro'

cxxvii

some god blinded by his own cigarette smoke
in his white ire gave us this pause of light
this brief circumference of sparks and dun
a hill to traverse by night a fog to penetrate
a city visible for a moment only and battles
to scar the lapsing skin with enigmatic marks
euphoria of the hour ! statues of shadows
and the many silences perforated by sleep
does it then ? do we ask wondering why
across a single blade of grass summer lilts
the heat folds and the form of writing dust
when *Lady-of-the-Flowers* comes to gather
hues from the purpling blooms and heather
the faces of the recondite many who have
gone before and the labyrinthine garden
which is a tomb a crepuscular distance
where ghosts flit looking for speech acts
involved wheels brightness of flares breath
and the horses of the sun blazing and swart
distinctions between consciousness and inert
the rock formed over night standing in the way
this is the grammar and rhetoric of dew
vanishing before it can become a secret

it is love poetry in the Sicilian dialect and
tone and accent and the string of vowels
pronounced over the glittering afternoon sea
when the telephone will be invented and
divinities hitherto undetected loud semaphores
a traffic of skies in collision the ephemera
and phenomena of clouds lying on their backs
trying to read the thoughts of earthly children
Pasargadae ! its gates flung open and lions
and leopards bearing the royal mane of kings
proceed pulling chariots of molten gold
all in an instant and the nightingale song of
the body uncontained in its sudden music
the dizzy swarm of mind plunging sweet
into the stairwell where the god awaits
with his cigarette and ineffable gaze
and darkness the all surrounding

cxxviii

trains blades knives and swords
fill the head subliminal hemispheres
of the sun turning bronze on the back
of an afternoon hill to the west of memory
the body in its immemorial death and waters
darkening in the swift flash of a metal
that endows mortality on statues and
shadows the lichen and moss underfoot
the tree trunk leaning against the rays
of a declining hour and the sea-murmur
in the ear of rock deposited by the edge
of a field rustling with empires of insects
black and red ants in a duel to the death
and fingers and mugs of ice cold substance
and the eye in a fever trying to gather

what it can of the vanishing horizon
war zones dividing dream from reality
zing and zoom and the glass inverted
that retains for a brief instant the light
if only a hand could take it and extend
its eternity into the oncoming darkness
underscored by human frailty sleep
develops long integers of dusk and dim
contours shifting in unheard speech acts
vowel submits to vowel and a wing
circling in the overhead sky of illusion
red myth imprinted on the x-ray screen
the corporeal suddenly becomes unconscious
whatever there was of the touch of grass
of the slow engines that operate the air
winds in the shapes of ink and sand
that come rushing to absolve matter
of its ego and the thunder ! of distance
the head grown too heavy sinks deep
into the infinite Etruscan night

cxxix *(a ballad)*

Joe is by far the oldest person known
the ministers of death have seen to that
the bracken hiatus of a million years
and when girls came into being
on a field of autumn gold and rain running
as if never seen before and through trees
took with their laughter Joe's young soul
a piano a drum and a snare the song
he played through their wild hair
gambling cards and voluptuous trumpet notes
hard and heavy the winter dense arrived
the jostle of frost against argent panes

Joe's time increased and his burning vowel
mystery and symmetry of outer-space
he learned to ken and wrote in back-hand
the book of *Transformations* in a trice
blow down the house ! secret lore is in the leaves
dice cast and cast again the pools blacken
and high among the tangled branches
his drunken soul contend
and so it was and wore his sleeves in hues
of western hills and tempest in the dew
but those girls eternity was in their fleeting kiss
and Joe now a Mayan prophet god a spin
and fabric of ardent bright in robes
of universal peace his childhood a remote
fan a marble relic of the Parthenon
and I ever at his side a shadow and flick
of verse and oriental fingertips
confusion of speech and silence a tongue
vibrating in the sleep of centuries
his dream I shared his antipathies and maps
but far from the ancient mountain far
from the zigzagging riverbed of an afternoon
spent with dragon-flies in motionless summer heat
great circles and a perimeter of sparkling dust
the chronometer on the kitchen wall
the lawn waiting to be mown
garage and basement smelling of gasoline and rust
paired by some god at birth to unfold the years
yet a thousand miles from his unexpected pyre
I learned the burden of unearned solitude
a hundred years and more the echo of his voice
and twenty times that the imprint of his loss
a small hand waving in a concrete wind
ave atque vale and farewell
and those girls eternity was in their fleeting kiss

cxxx

the ancient poets ! how did the great sun
appear to them through mossy crevice
and passionate desire – the world in robes
and rock and the trees that line the mind
and the reverie and being stunned with loss
the mire and swamp of constant despair
was the great sun *love* to them and did ire
and the metals of yearning and rejection
the phosphorous of inclement days and
weathers of absence and stoned amazement
pit them against tempests of understanding ?
this day is allotted to them the scribblers
of recondite *amore* in romance dialects
spoken only in the moon's archaic vestibule
their similes and metaphors of drowning
and wasting in ciphers of marble estuaries
half-broken off from earths of pleasure
and sobbing into sleeves of dark portent
the ancient poets ! they are with us still
zodiacal and oblivious of the afternoon's
long decline in a storm of grass and weeds
and searching for the foot and ankle
of a beloved who wears only jewels their
smart and ache their dolorous refrains
that stain the passing hour with vowels
lachrymose and unheard to the common ear
does sleep capture them in its brief eternity ?
how do they travel now from Mexico to
the fierce unknown with a baggage of letters
riveting hieroglyphs wedges and chisels
and waxen tablets and enormous routines
in a late Latin of truncated syllable and tone
the foreigner is prince in this sorrowing
and grief on its foot-stools panders derelict

to emotions of illegal heart-ache and death
the night-sky opens its ruddy curtains letting
in the sheen of eternal star-weft the bright
that can only wound and hopelessness of
recurring breath and distances of mountain
and rapturous sea-shrill of missing birds
wing and cheek and briar that cuts to
the marrow of love's feigned distend alas
the ancient poets ! *Cavalcanti* and *Rudel*
lesions in waters of a postponed dawn
dew and inks that pour from the brow
unwritten lessons in chalk and smoke

a hand could never crave so much as
the design the shadow makes in death

cxxxi

this is not how I remember being
Max but is there any other way ?
the tree in its incredulous beauty
beside the stone that prevents the road
from moving and rains and bees and
air in clusters of invisible knots and
the height and breadth depth and width
of the solitary thought of light and
skies moving rapidly from dawn to twilight
the length of a single day in childhood
eternity wrapped in a spear of grass
distance of a voice yelling to come home
margins of water on the opposite side
of sleep and the small incident of fever
like a death in the first instance unexpected
as the removal of hands in the dark
not recalling where the body is when
it wakes in a different unknown world

floor and ceiling and maps of walls
circulating only in one of two eyes
and what of words their lack of
meaning and shape a volley of sounds
vowels ricocheting on a plastic keyboard
the voluminous effort to reconstruct
the pattern of language on a screen
devoid of color's digital memory
one two or three the improbable order
of counting when an hour has no end
what did it mean to go to the store
profusion and variety of cans and shelves
a car lot music zooming from above
inability of spoons and forks to act
coming and going up and down elevators
and offices of immaculate despair
did it never want to go somewhere else
a lake of ribbons and silt and greenery
crossing a rattle trap bridge of slats
to walk again ! murmur of hidden dots
and insects that intersect the mind
with promises of intellect and flight
a wonder to remove the switch and listen
humming buzz and whine of unwanted
larger people it seems in starched hues
and beds that talk in the middle of the night
it had to end somehow these trips of
round and round trying to breathe just
right and unnumbered selves yes
the extraordinary last time it happened
as sudden as the first time to die
time no longer than its only century
and windows that disappear in space
goodbye kaleidoscope of life !

cxxxii

NO NEED FOR RELIGIONS
for temples commas or hiatuses
poetry is just the lack of reason
the spinning out of the unspun
the river that talks in both directions
a simplex and a mustard seed
and a mountain that never was
NO NEED FOR METAPHYSICS
an altar for the disbelieving
a grass lot a cribbed reduct
the place where water goes at night
the holy and unholy both
mouthed while sleeping under
and the roof and sequence of walls
and stucco beds and native plays
the birth of no one to be celebrated
NO NEED FOR AFTERTHOUGHTS
just the knee in spasm a shoulder
that weeps hearing a poem reversed
the words in woof and weft
a vowel destroyed by leaves
whoever thinks otherwise
in workshops of organized religion
or stops because the traffic does
and never questions why
poetry is of the distant sea
waves anarchic with light that rise
a breath in surfeit a death surmise
who never did what mother said
denying thrice his master's voice
ALIVE

cxxxiii

the once and the twice and *forevermore*
whatever happened over there the accident
and none who recall that swans were lifted
invisibly by poetry into a distance of
unseen skies enormous cloud fragments
framework of x-ray and words in scrambled
Spanish beside a hindu temple five thousand
stories high and monks with Dravidian names
and foreclosures on mortgages and bank riots
south of Peru and gamesters and cock-fights
inglorious wagers thumbs down and the world
was an anvil the gods beat with drums of heat
that captured the human mind in circles
of regret and passion and mimesis of thought
how many flowers in a foot print ?
it was a headache and in a trice the days
turned to crystal impenetrable and beautiful
ear-rings and anklets and epic verses about
loss peregrine flights of unnamed birds
recitations in the void and star-rise of intellect
jeopardy of mind in its dual function
dying to the real-estate of emotion and flung
afar the syllables of hope the restraints and leashes
why do we keep surmising it can return ?
envelopes arrive secretly at night packed
with hair and small quicksilver rings
and automobiles with no memory purr
through canyons and the radio is big and loud
and voices over-dubbed of deities in song
crash courses in electronics and software
and quantum mechanics inverted by the rose
petal by petal the fate of the mortal soul
unfolds buzzing receptacles where detritus
and tragedy cumulate their untold tales

and in myriads of vowels the empyrean discloses
an afterworld haunted by the children we once were
and grass and leaf and rock and dragonflies
that flit above the river of an enigmatic afternoon
hives and colored swaths of air bright at first
then like dun hills fade into Hesperian longing
that springs from Minerva's hidden brow
a jet of water illusions of history books
speeches and derisive oratory on a mound
where the buried of the Trojan wars fester
lotus and jasmine and basalt black as night
the ends of things digits and dots the inch
of space the ear of stone the locked circumflex
that lingers over an echo circling *forevermore*

cxxxiv

because the cavern is where the blind can see
and red is all they crave and because water
runs its course in a solitary ditch the heights
are never pure and fever races to the grave
on its hundred degrees of feet and whatever
else you might conclude the world's but a
grain of sand a midge can push and sleep
is the weight that brings the body down
like a feather in disguise and isn't it ordinary
that poetry is incomplete that the meaning
is in the enigma and hospitals fill with ether
and language is a boat carved out of stone
my hands can speak no more my eyes have
vowels inside that circle the empyrean's ink
star after star crashes in the pool of time
and Caesar and his secret bride of hieroglyphs
strut with pride on the sandy strip to die
angels with inverted wings and paragraphs

that rhyme with light what more is there
to say circles ciphers zeroes and omicrons
the sky to sing when day is done the child
with half a mind has gone his lonely way

cxxxv

solo for missing voices

books to read people to see flights to catch !
abstract city of mirrors where night goes
and reflections in a wind-mill fire and brass
stains that orient the sky toward its apocalypse
collisions of black-holes ! all in a single minute
refer to the footnotes in the palimpsest and
weep Brother the time is nigh and hunters
with microbial emerald eyes on the stalk
for traces of the dead in sheets and pillows
yellowing with an abject memory of weeping
so little the time that remains and fossil ideas
to keep us going though the page has burned
its last indications and a remote asterisk
marks the hour's improbable mid-point
whence the epic makes its wild start tempests
winds with human voices hands of clouds loud
intimations of skin no less and the junction where
ink and reason intersect writing words with false
etymologies and the stars that glow at midday
menacing attributes of fate and of each mortal
the formal decay of time a plenitude of atmospheres
to drown ! the boats set sail from their rock
that can never be but in the incomplete stanzas
dimly recalled of missing vowels interjections of
air and light and the vast moving mountain west
of the horizon and the sayings of ancient oracles
azure tinted frames spectra that copulate in glass

and the long winches of the bedding as it drifts
into soft mattresses of water blacker than pitch
an aura of sound the haunting echo of dew as
it braids its wistful hair around the grass
it is dawn ! far reach of birth even as fingers
lost in the maze of a childhood lawn prepare
the soul for its flight from the confused stage
where mask and identity propound their entelechy
medley of insane proclivities toward the *gone*
a sad longing leaf shaking dark the silence

cxxxvi

to wonder is the mirror of the poem
a river of phantoms that pass no
sooner glimpsed from view a sleep
they enter like into water to drown
effigies of memory the length of an echo
the poem crystallizes a river of wonder
where phantoms drown in their sleep
perhaps never to wake again unless as
verses of the poem brought together
by echoes of light and distance a wonder
simply moving as water does underneath
the mind's imperfect memory of the poem
the cosmic innerness of the vast outside
river and echo mirror and glass in which
phantoms that we are dance and drown
in the poem as it moves a river of light
++++++++++++++++++++++++++++++
famous structures and weight of the poem
enduring through material obstacles
farflung destinies gods thundering oaths
and threats to all dimensions of the poem
under and over in sheets of language

bipolar and bejeweled with obsidian vowels
the matter of nature and nature of matter !
excrescences on the skin of space as it
revolves evolving out of the fluid context
of the poem the riverrun of eternity a dream
within the mirror of dreams unraveling
reflections and shadows and echoes of space
poem of viscera and heroes and mountains
that do battle with infinity and rocks
interspersed like consonants in the feminine
syntax of the poem loud and soft wide-hipped
broad-eyed the laughter of women-girls
reciting in the courtyard the massive poem
one by one in the tangled labyrinth of memory
glass and inside glass the rutilating stars
playing the part of symbols and immense
compound nouns and fractures of number
reverberating in the mirror's profound ear
digital swarms of bees eye-sequences of color
unseen and invisible the characters in
a script of mask and ego running by water's
edge into a mirror of smoke and legend
the poem ! cosmic interruption of light
a man's life is the poem and even more so
a man's death is the totality of the poem
++++++++++++++++++++++++++++++++++
epic poem ! marvel of the unconscious
seed and germ of the only day that ever was
plenitude and vacuum of the poem the all-
absorbing and circulating heat of the sun's
embryo black and enormous in the afternoon
of the mirror back and forth pitch and call
green reverie of leaf and grass ultimatum
of sweet hives drenched in a basalt pool
the poem ! to be remembered and

forgotten daily hourly by the minute

instantantaneous reconditioning !

cxxxvii

what remains is a mystery of opaline dust
silent catastrophe of worn out batteries
or small jewels broken by a high fever
the entire universe shaking in a single leaf
speechless as incomplete statues absorbed
contemplating the sky's forbidden azure
room after room of undisclosed documents
doors ceilings windows chairs reversed and
the hallucinatory remnants of a caged pet
the fleet the fast the foot of racing time
the never more of again will this return
how much the house is not a home the sad
unrelenting wheel of invisibility that turns
heat and wild the tryst of cloud and rain
voyage of three thousand miles of mountain
until ash and rust resolve the dim refrain
has a hand thus quenched the cycling burn
a brain shelved in unequal galaxies each
a hemisphere on its own the restless and
loss of speech tongue the rattle insecure
traveler without a route a caped destiny
mask and fringe the spectral childhood
revisited how many times and never past
the tenth solar year a frieze in the wind
summer's dolorous end in a dented horn
the red box the lesser deities share at night
basement of transfigurations and omicron
ghostly silhouette passing through glass
come midnight when motors turn to god
abracadabra of the windmill sawing

threats and flung the antipodal vowels
can so much misconstrued memory be
at its terminus the x-ray and mercury
band-aids and pewter dishes disarray
day after day the promise to come home
broken against the slanted light that
disfigures eternity's brief afternoon

cxxxviii

what's to know about the moon
quartered by girls carrying baskets
to altars of the dark goddess who has lain
in furrows and drawn the tide around
her waist and signified and lightened
the moon growing dim and ruddy
and the girls loosening their tresses
weaving heat and distances of fire
through their intense summer vowels
night ! serenity and duplicity both
issuing from the moon's secret eye
like a thread becoming liquid argent
rills running over smooth pebbles
when no one is looking and the drug
taken to sleep and the immense whiteness
that absorbs the consonants of oblivion
girls ! enchanting and deadly
dancing allurements on a porch screened
off from fireflies who devastate
and other insects that infect the ear
and by day what of the moon asleep
in sheets of seraphic silk colorless and
embroidered with unseen memories of
the dark goddess her rivers and caves
and immense hidden fields spreading

to the south where the gone encamp
haunted by the moon in its least
transformations and ready to apportion
impermanent death to leaf and rock
bathed in the moon's intense reflection
mirror and backside quicksilver and
crystal impenetrable lunar syllables
and the dark goddess on the chase
red-eyed and swift splitting in half
her quarry a meandering human soul
that tarried too long in the dangers of light
and what of the moon-rise on the hill
things undone and never seen
far distant the shades of ether
dissolving the five elements
into dewy starless night

cxxxix

air carved into components of heat
drill and rock components of mind
thought in a pair of pillars
rising from scorched dust the abyss
of history in letters erased by a tumult
of hands divisive and abstract vowels
memorized and stamped in cursive script
drawn out over the fluid contexts of sleep
such as it is the story of mankind
encapsulated in a few brief verses
stochastic and chronological only in the barest
of senses the serpent in versions of myth
interwoven in labyrinthine recensions
a perceived distance brought near
through acts of mirror and speech
statuary come into being fully conscious

and gods abruptly visible for a moment only
cinema and reduction of the stage
footprint warp and woof small gardens
trampled by the elephant of epic
the mahout on his back arrayed in hues
twelve times brighter than the sun
and the lamps of paradise circling
the dreamer in his weft of dappled sounds
will I ever wake from this hiatus ?
chaos and jargon of information
fill the brain with a rushing cement of illusion
hospitals and decks of littered beds
the balcony of time suspended above
magma and primordial miasma
sent out from the missing center star-stuff
babble of origins black holes and red dwarfs
every day this happens once or twice
men rattled over appearance of mice
clouds of insects summers of loudness
drum roll and fife in the shattered ear
and the children from out of nowhere
running to play with leaves and pools
darkness that takes them within the hour
densities of infinity in a single blade of grass
mahabharatas of unending argument
in the tangled twilight of language
here and there the abracadabra of echoes
issuing from stone fragments
the great disorder of hills
longing and melancholy
shadows

cxl

in the name of the loud the grief and the heart-stricken
we x-ray Thee this way thrice wise a sky blooming
for a cloud-dress and numberless too the angel-rays
light ! assumed ascending the soul in and of itself
gossamer tapestries of the freed-from-thought Bliss !
checkered flights wings a-whirr and wasn't he a tad
of a boy a fling on the lawn with colored and over
such running through hoops and sugar-licks red
and striped and like the weather of a flimsy april day
june and july were the heated worst in suits overlaid
sweating until everything became unsewn the livid
spits the quid draining through the air-holes and pleat
and plastered the surgeon in his Turkish gown a-strut
with hammer and tongs yes to everything possible
but no promises as to the quantity of life as he rarely
put it a digit at a time referencing pronouns in the abstract
when the punctuation was over and delivered by spoons
to the weary of roadside stitching the woods in their
poison green depths and even distances roseate limbed
a god could be haunting and by noon which lasted several
months lunations of gravity on hold and speech a thong
in width and spark however wasn't that a lesson sorrowing
drew maps of the flight-pattern the looking back the thumb
in appraisal and the parts of the hand once applauded for
their vowels weaving the ink inner to grasses the union
of air and ether the marriage of mercury and Toledo
fission beyond what the body can take no wonder a lung
at a time the rhombus and buzz the hive and humming
sadder as each day proves the last is here the one to dread
called a long time to the sirens a bell a bong a whistle
delved sea-moats heights furze and bellows the anvil
here lay the head's remains a thought turning blue
oxygen ! hiatus and aphasia skin's undetermined song
unforgettable

cxli
luna llena

whose gold-tipped stone sharpened arrows are these ?
handed down from the time of Brahma through warrior
caste and to whet the taste for blood in battles alike
with god demon and mortal and now lay scattered
on demesnes of dust under domes of cerulean ether
a curious silence of wind and branch a rag hanging
from leaf-tip and speech broken in unequal moan
and sigh the vowels cast like discarded fingers to the dew
can ask but no ear contain the answer and hilts carved
from elephant tusk and shapely as the memory of dance
and the narrow-waisted girls who appeared at dusk
among overturned tables shattered wine goblets a mirror
holding night as prey and the glittering encrustations of
planets rising slowly over dim western hills and whose
massive sword razor sharp on either hemisphere and
crying in the trampled grass and flowers distributed
on garlands draped over drunken throats sobbing
can so many have so thoughtlessly plunged into the fray
linking syllable to syllable in wrath and stoking ash
and root the slept soliloquy of the dark goddess her
raiment and sash torn and fouled ancient as her hair
a poisoned storm flashing in the deliberation of kings
petty insects covered in gold-flake making claim
to fields and distances and seas they have never seen
but only silence establishes its haunted gilded moon
over the rusting weaponry and earth tilts into a ditch
forlorn with sluggish water and echo of foot-falls
nocturnal remains of a poetry now turned to saliva
coarse and guttural consonants shadow sounds of
desperate metals clank and opprobrium the burning
sloth and envy of politicians cankered with greed and ire
whose arms stored in vast water tanks or under foot
can hear now the roaring the blasted final note

how archaic stone becomes rot and mulch and soft
as the children were now spent and nameless tombs

cxlii
pomp and circumstance

the thin divide between time and eternity
where a device in the ear turned on makes loud
and at times a devastating white and all memory
is silence along a horizon that only distinguishes night
from night a longing to ache the time before last
birthright of stone and leaf monogram of light
embossed in a small pink shell on the shores of space
is heard no more than a remote whiz a buzzing
in the sleeping grass on darkened lawns of oblivion
you ask and no one answers a door opens and shuts
a path out leads to the dense wood of poisoned
greenery the unknown and baffling stanzas that
sing in a language yet to be invented a sequence
of infernal beauties in syllables argent and unheard
such beatitude in the buried archaic world
volumes of cloud dense and rolling over the oracle
sleeping and adrift in domains of distant ether
you step and without knowing enter the other world
a dazzle of gong and blitz and sheets lain over
recondite figures a statuary of fog and mist
masks that live on pearl and oriental gemstones
grimoire and lattice shaking slightly in the dawn
a roseate breeze articulations of the ineffable
blooming like sparks of an insectary behind glass
come ! heralds of finger and whetstone beckon
you have nowhere to turn you are an adolescent
sudden and evolving somewhere between a library
and the abandoned wheel of misspent destiny
++

strings of the names of gods extend into infinity a
bang a bangle a smashing of coppers and brasses
armor burning in small heaps beside the designations
for heroes in various Neolithic tongues AyEE !
you are between darkness and greater darkness
a brief script in your hand wearing pantaloons
full of zephyrus and bright green camisole and a brother
like you in size and ink fomenting dimensions in a
southerly direction a friction between alpha and gamma
islands suddenly endowed with feet and seas raving
at noon the boiling point of history in the drugstore
where emphatic marks of punctuation redden intensely
you are there with girlfriend a rage in her ypsilon shaped
eyes and both are waiting for the sad bus of beyond
to transport you past the brick works of mind the
salt and pepper asphalt of a summer vacation in Hades
and soon the graft and drift of a tectonic age some
call Kali Yuga and smarting from the light you
all spine erect and somehow smaller than when born
a hospital with wings ! situations of the irreversible !
the twin and his adjunct in quicksilver suits heated
and disputing the point of no return at high school
graduation which is in fact a funeral with horns
foot-ware uncomfortable distinctions between
psyche and plumbing cliffs and head-gear zing !
your adolescent self standing there a-quiver

the thin divide between time and eternity

cxliii

it was nice when the sun came up
and to be afloat on the sea of dreams
they came and went laughter and light
a season among the statues of thought
a random and then vanishing moment

in the chance of asterisk and comma
heavenly bodies of just once in the skies
night and trees and a road unknown
stone that marks the end of the future
on either side of the house a question
of lawns and heat and wild bird-calls
come home !

cxliv

chill in the descent of the following words
oriental dispassion at the unknown tomb
of the poet in disguise all saffron and robe
cumulation of cloudbursts in the eye and
summer as the definition of the all in a life
disregarded by god and snake alike dust
and opprobrium nickel-ware choices afar
fields and the mountain only for its weight
sifted like red powder in the hoodoo of time
a lesser known deity in her stormy hair
capsized like a boat in ice the night before
and singing loud and great the fuming
dictator of Olympus charged by fish
electrified and boomed from the first
by a tragic incomplete premonition aleph
and digitalized betas the whole array seized
by a single finger and worn like grass over
the wound wasn't that a sorrow a given
to grief a session with a medium half-blind
with cognition and the sleep in parts of
the intervening letters delta and the like
soporific as pharaohs after dinner who
are climbing a dream scale of music who
cannot be invited again to the lexicon
who are hard by the well this afternoon

or going to the library but cannot get there
a grammar including the brahmanic idiom
then evening brings its hills to bear and
the whole twilit sky and of course listening
to the radio for the funeral and its somber
drum and clapper and crackling the noise
of a theater of thunder soft but deafening
sitting side by side the twin in his fabric
of june july and august ready to burn

cxlv

a summer afternoon

a movie of the sky it lasted for hours
turning violet then racing purple diminished
into attitudes darkening more intensely until
the treetops were swept away and the hero
or a god ravished in a poisonous green glare
appeared like an idol of crumbling stone
in the afternoon downpour and what remained
of childhood the small budding utopias of ivy
or ant hills or the grass grown too long
in its hour of perpetual noon when we mapped
the minutes of echo and lay forgotten beneath
the sun's lavish pagoda of yellow streamers
who was the first to move from his seat
and walk stunned into the bellows where heat
circulated with a violence that takes the breath
and following who came second wondering
at the universe of bees as they whirled humming
above in airy epics of saturation and death
no matter the day lingered in a format of hills
of towpaths and riverbanks of isolation
from mind and the eternal vacuum of light
briefly the dragonfly stationed forever

above the water radiated its pale mauve essence
and a Byzantium of trees shuddered slightly
waiting for a scimitar to cut them down and for
a full moon to bless their dense kingdoms
and there by the sluggish vapid stream
stirred dreams of the other life of the place
where memory has no value and rock
jutting out from the boundaries of time
resembles nothing more than infinite sleep
and sky just born immense higher than ever
unattainable as we lay our twin corpse to rest
flowers and curlicues and truncated hands
drawing circles in the vast multiple air

cxlvi

what is history ? hordes of winged termites
heading for the Taj Mahal !
and what happens after the end of time ?
jasmine and porphyry in profusion
hues that decorate the terminus of space
so many still sleeping or already gone
the finger and the child that belongs to it
the glass inside which memory places us
small integers trying to decipher the squiggles
in a book of pictures and maps meant
to represent the origins of the cosmos
you blow into my ear ! and in that whisper
which is the promise of the transitory
I see the battlefield arrayed with sumptuous
phalanxes and banners and monkeys screeching
elephant and horse and chariot in a riot
before all turns to dust and the motley sun
suspended like an erratic yellow dot
in the varieties of azure and cloud rot

drifting above the house where we sat
for hours in a daze confused by a single word
or a syllable or the slightest blade of grass
struggling to decipher a myth
something that happened in the hiatus
between statue and living breath a vision
without images and yet stepping forth
out of rock the blank Persephone
whiter than white & her cinnamon-colored eyes
a trance with figure-eights dancing
among the hushed leaves of an eternity
what was the human voice in that lunation ?
orphic cry resounding in the petrified trees
a remnant of cloth a divinity in fragments
scattered on the path leading out of Hades
++++++++++++++++++++++++++++++++++
what is history ? the
inchiostro wasted in
naming the stars

cxlvii

where the hand is where the head is
the heart is the shape memory gives
fossils that looming write large
script over waters running darkly
beside the opposite bank of the river
is it a tree that yearns or the cloud
gracing some ephemeral distance
we are plunged in masses of night
stark formulas and clamors for
a past of erroneous oils and shifts
star beams swifter than arrows
ears lips ribs and ankles hypnotized
whose body and at what hour is zero

rushing to and fro of noon heat
lightened only by a statue's monopoly
of silence adrift in a poetry written
in backhand with mirror diacritics
and a length of air you can breathe
for just a minute before the machine
takes over in some dense green room
whir and chirp of nocturnal insects
and the sudden perforation of space
through which are seen myriads of
nameless star entities either falling
or seeking a way out of the grammar
that put them there in the first place
I am Orestes ! the claudicating comet
infers dying to the point of no return
a season on earth was too much
anvil and cemetery and oblique cars
transporting parts of mind back to
their origins dusty hill slopes behind
whatever the eye can perceive in a day
so long it says in a vedic dialect all
signatures and the unpronounceable
vowel and accent the hiatus where
we find ourselves today forms of air
aspects of ether and longing the sad
tow path through lean twilight grasses
a home on the verge of lamps and
cycles of hair and the immensity
out there we cannot understand

cxlviii

the milk at the end of the run in a sky
of clouds in a burst of summer the thread
has no connection to the void and yet

and yet we et cetera down here in the grass
between wars a simple pile of bones a heap
ants haul away crumb by crumb call it
as we do often or not enough a semantics
of loss and grief the outbursts of rain
purplish darkening the minute of hours
awful sense of done it before of known it
from somewhere else of riding the mountain
to its etymological origins in the sea the
great topaz and emerald sea with its jasper
reflections and the sun an imminent ball
of destruction haze and song and lip
blistered by its own echo I can't come back
to the place where it seemed so sweet the real
the ineffable dot dot dot on the bottom line
sign and it's all yours flashy metal and
stucco wall and fence zigzagging up the myth
and back OK lie down do it again if you want
gas and stars and masses of woman-hair
like a storm in the tropics of a dream you
in the middle and water and air and the
you know the rest elements both Greek and
Sanskrit in nature they call it *phainoumena*
pronominal effect of sleep each knee on
its bolt and the surf coming in fast and high
turn it off ! legend of rock formations
nostalgic vowels leaves intimate in their
language and dying to remember why and
who went first and the gravel path and colored
stones on either side and father in his usual
irate mood swinging left and right the glass
imagery of gods thirty three to be exact
in their massive jewel ornamented cars staring
just staring down at us woebegone stiffs
careless in our suits of make believe and a radio

a person in music and drifting silently away
so long to the yesterday a life it was
piece by piece the tattered cloth caught
on the briar and the pit down below and

cxlix

the latin brick the greek stain the endless
how much longer will it take
at one end the embroidery come apart
frayed the beautiful and plangent
the undotted iotas of exclamatory dejection
the hypothesis of the sun unraveling
around the moon the headstone that marks
what never should have happened I know
this is futile the library books the card files
the learning and more learning erudition
at the other end the pieces of glass and
the small photographic detail and grass
like hair in the wild afternoon wind
will never come back the many gone the
mourned unforgotten what matter
my life's remains against this dust and
echelons of sky and nightfall and mind
fractured and set into urns as ancient as
water and the planet crazy wobbling off course
burning burning as in the scriptures intended
to self-destruct and what each layer of sound
means each vowel in its place vanishing
into the eerie spaces of air where planets
go to die and the black solar flares and heights
of religious thought steaming chaotically
to spend the last of one's years in solitude
driving around in insane circles looking
for that section of memory that piece of light

that emblem and saturation of love that
whatever else happened was life a moment
or two dancing with fireflies and soft
the place where the head goes down and
sleep at last like stone configured
for its eternal hour of silence I am that going
too among asphodel and phlox and ginger-root
a finger here a finger there and like
a transformation of matter into pure energy
dissolving fractioned into miniature worlds
gone too I am with the patterns and designs
of entelechy and the unheard poetry
of desire I once was that and passionate
the consonant in the very middle pronounced
like aspiration and declamation and rotating
numb and undetected the rest of the poem
the cliffs of Sanskrit conjuncts a *cry !*
famous elephants of the gods bruiting
loud their brassy shlokas reverberating
like tympana of rushing leaves through the ear
and I too gone with the least of these tones
with the dulled accent with the whisper
borrowed from my dying brother the least
shade of indifference the parasol and stick
going back to school with kids deader than ever
and shouting and playing and the earth's
unconjectured mass imploding and the eye
the distance that contains it the last
and final thing seen and unseen
whom I loved

cl

take this east and make it west
take this north and make it south

the gods who eat waves are at the door
asking for the suburb they gave you
to inhabit the light they gave you
to wonder and now they want your breath
as well and the paintings on the walls
the abstracts in stucco and ink the grief
and sorrow hidden in the envelope
and the hair of the women you loved and
come nightfall and the sounds of motors
from afar burrowing in the great cavity
of silence and the rest of space like a brief
indentation into the one thought remaining
of giving in to darkness and its dozen myths
the gods all thirty three who eat waves
and make soliloquys in clouds are at the door
asking for the children they loaned you
and the house and the rugs and rags
and even your sleep they want back
the world is tinsel dangling in your eye
a shred of bone some lint dead ants
wherever you look the math of some lost game
unravels its enigmatic numbers in the glass
frenzied you search your conscience
for the mistake you made
when you said *Yes*

cli
países vastos como el insomnio
Octavio Paz

the *light* buzzes alive with memory
cutting through voices of the leaves
that never seem to sleep in this country
riddled with centuries of oblivion even
as I enter the errant wood and shadow

a Dante of complex vowels and unsure
of foot over rock and glide the waters
swift bringing to the ear such tones as
scramble the mind in its perplexity
assume today is the last of Wednesdays
market open one more time awnings aflutter
does blood run down the gutters and meat
flailed corpses of game dangle upside down
do the paving stones begin to talk and
call out for surgeons to excise the *light* ?
this Dante , me ! protracted shadow
lost in an Umbria of despair unable more
to count the lives gone by missing allure
of faces in a rush of quickened terra cotta
hills that lumber slowly to certain doom
sciences of number and cosmology above
in the fabricated sky of *trecento* poetry
angelic hosts with blazing weaponry
in flight through a string of zeroes
am I to recount the thread that passes
through the dying eye and call that
the architrave of mystery ? one soul alone
is all the souls I have ever lost and still
the day is done no sooner dawn starts
its wan trumpet of flares and cock's crow
and the fields below bathed in ocher
seem to tremble under phantom beasts
white as the plagiary of desire and lowing
muffled identities of Pythagorean thought
do I resemble these as much as anything
hide to be flailed and breath in spurts
of frosty air the everlasting morning which
brings me up to date the *now* evanescent
and darker still a realm where hands
undesigned yearn to open secret doors

here is me a Dante of absences and fear
identity laid out on ancient paving stones
mosaic obliterated on disappearing walls
exiled from a Florence of pure infancy
a rill in the argent flows of Arcadia
a beam borrowed from a lunar whisper
a nothing sawed in half by starlight !
a night of cloaks and feathered bedding
a mind of unequal hemispheres listing
like the proverbial boat on the storms
arms upraised to receive enigmatic music
shares of infinite diapason and lutes
that strike notes in medieval Arabic
a message from the Prophet a syllable
incandescent with trails of longing
white and black Beatrice and Cavalcanti
whom I will ever mourn though this day
has but a single hour and all the rest
is interred beside a cathedral of dark fire
insomnia holds me always in its grip
a distance of mountains endless dust
a landscape pocked with all my griefs

clii

before the beginnings of words their endings
like rivers without source all madly pouring
dusts powders clouds mists the antithesis
of matter the doubt of light the fraction
of a vowel inserted in the hiatus of a poem
yet to be written yet to be put in stone asleep
the decibels of zero and infinity combined
to form the question mark that starts all
discourse a phantom reason an abracadabra
of statues learning to talk though speech

acts have been abolished and aphasia reigns
three thousand one hundred and thirty three
the number of gods dancing on a single sun-ray
seeds sands and the oceans contained in one
enormous wave fictions of language descriptors
green and gold and lurid backdrops of hair
unkempt savage storms swirling combs glass
the size of ink and stars raining down like dew
all that the eye embraces sleeping !
do we dare go on another step a plunge off
the cliff of logic riding a single-wheeled chariot
mad to have at the nebulous goddess of tongues
waist and heights of knee and sublimities of ankle
unique system of weights and measures gravity
hands that remove themselves from mirrors
galaxies upended on a single note of grief
howling from the distant within of the heart
tears unexpurgated texts of sorrow enigmatic
as alphabets of crystal buried in non-existent hills
the west of opprobrium x-rays of dorsal love
to have lost everything repeatedly in pronunciation
and remember nothing of the irreversible moment
insects of mortality ! a knife a cup a noontime
forever extended beyond the horse's hoof
into the median of passions when the poem
finally resurrects that most intimate emotion
depth ! it is never loud enough in rock shaping
words again and again out of the cubicle of air
wherever we go only ruin life in death
inches from the birth of time
leaves remembering

cliii

between two knees struggling to remember
I saw death a river of light extinguished
by a single finger and the immensities
of everything else eclipsed in the wink of an eye
you were gone in the disregarded moment when sand
rushes to merge with all the unknown seas
the blank and the white and the invisible green ones
where shoulders drown and nothing but a small
conjunction a hiatus that separates thought
from mind soul from flesh sight from memory
how else to explain the empty days that followed
sequence of ink and storm and torn leaf
craving for sleep inside a rock beside a road
that travels infinitely nowhere
touching the remains of fever on your spine
holding something inert and yet familiar
I knew death as the instantaneous universe
that pivots in an insect's eye sure and definite
as the blade of grass that feeds it and then
it was no more walls trembling a buzzing
in the vacuum left when the air disappeared
the intimate vowel that could not be inserted anywhere
filling the ear with the echo of night
upside down and all around the least intimation
of the day before when worlds and earths
riding in their crazy ambulance still seemed
alive

cliv

wake up ! it can't be slept all day
light and all its suburbs at the window
graceful mountain nymphs in gauze
rippling as waves in the dawning air

wake up ! it can't be slept all day
Morpheus is tired of your embrace
and wants you forth a liquid element
to dazzle in the sun's wanton rays
horse of glistening movements tethered
to memory and the springs and lacks
plateaus and all-devouring pools
so deep nothing in them ever returns
wake up ! it can't be slept all day
the Mahabharata has yet to be read
and spilled like cascades over jungles
of unexplored Deccan the verses one
million strong and in length distance
to the moon in hallucinating epicycles
the day has not been invented that
will hold your leaping soul aloft
nor counted the mourning beings
left behind on this infirm cliff-ledge
wake up ! it can't be slept all day
iridescent blue morning-glory !
hummingbirds in a wingéd blur
forever disappear in doubled light

Repetitions of the Invisible !

clv

I have revisited the structure of hell
and spoken with the bride of the underworld
cancer in all its triumphant graces and
the shadows that grow beneath fingernails
a witness to the power of night-flight
of renting rooms that do not exist
but for the fractions of things painted red
of signatures embossed on the missing page
of sulfur and grains that sprout from helium

indigenous vestibules sections of hair
unkempt as seas at midnight and above
and below the thin line of claustrophobia
the philosophies of cliff and death
is it no matter the past ceases to inform ?
where are the two cadavers that point north ?
what did the bride of the underworld mean
when she erected next to her skeleton
a map of Spain and its headwinds ?
whosoever walks through the ages
with only a finger broken in half
and speaks as if grass were immortal
whosoever will marry the unconscious bride
of the underworld and lacquer her nails
and orate to the Belt of Orion in Sudanese
let him have nothing back of the powers
but bury him on the next day in Provence
where Saint Dominick rides madness like a horse
glistening with noon and ivory and the endless
candles of despair riddled marble
questions of surgical half-moons
the child and the opposite of the child
hidden in a cell pumped by cyclotrons
nothing can ever be the same as the first time
only the leaf and its meal of black suns
the undergrowth of footprints leading
back to the cave and the hallucinatory sirens
gibberish of masts and ropes and flailing
how did I ever return from that tour
of hospitals and sick-bays and blood ordeals ?
I am not as before but as the reverse
of what the mirror holds captive
reflux of zeroes and their silent centuries
anatomy of enigma and dust

clvi

the bardic echo a faint aleph
burrowing in the worm's fossil ear
sound conveying heavens of distant rumor
waves the gods eat for lack of definition
and all the earths that burn between birth
and the imminent light-denying clause
an epiphany in the moment of self-
discovery just when the portals shut
is it grass clamoring for one more day ?
bright and suffused with a wan glare
that barely penetrates consciousness
the child abed with his dots and swirls
immersed in a mystery beyond his ken
can one minute only contain the entire
aftermath of sleep ? felled by a powdery
and invisible hand the small corpus of letters
plunges into a hinter-world of stone
where memory lies in ruins a marble
stained with centuries of inky error
gone the golden age ! gone the silver too
when a child lived a hundred years by
his mother's side innocent yet betrayed
now years are as pinpricks in obscurity
and outside of night's ramparts cries
of warriors agonized in a duel of science
and lunacy we are overwhelmed with
sheer emptiness and loss the dear ones
striven and cancelled from their X's
signatures in air and chanceries of wind
high thoughts about future lives
mere legends wrought by cunning gods
to further the following step the foot
that failed to run again the lessons
of ultraviolet and thimble and all art

gone wrong in the counterfeit of desire
if consciousness is but a small accident
of protein and chromosome what matters
the jejeune chemistry of love the leaf
and its passion to devour sunlight and
depthless seas where anemone and pod
struggle against vain crafts of darkness
tomorrow when bees will exist no more
and the hive symbol of that golden age
a dried husk and planets tumble from
their exercised paths into the chaos
which is beginning and end reversed !
still we wake and greet the day's first fiction
and walk as statues endowed with myth
and speak in volumes of poetry and cloud
how grief encumbers us instilling vowels
that seem like sacrosanct ascension into
the void and sorrowing extend our arms
into an ineffable yearning for infinity
though stunned and blind we see all that
has ever been and will never come again
the Saturday morning story hour the lapse
from knowledge the witless recognition
in the epiphany when doors open only
to shut again and a voice booms

don this armor and become dark !

clvii

an island in the sun a cliff a buffer
memory like a wind passing through light
leaves scoured the remains of things
in a trembling state of apostasy
we become then we cease ever it says
in echoing refrain on the margins

do you look at me do you hold up an arm
swarms of invisible winged creatures
our thoughts going out like cosmic gas
into a void we'll never know
being skin and optic nerve the senses
rally in our brains then crash sleeping
a lawn that stretches from birth
into the small inch of darkening loss
touch and response figures of love
the embrace and the chastisement
the human emotion to want to continue
becoming and feeling and yet shadows
is all we are and beneath circling trees
or on avenues of water rushing
to take us by the knees and we tumble
out of sight as if we'd never been

clviii

a clarity is within me large and bright odorless
and deep inside me too a non-existent world big
expanding with all the summers possible and waters
enormous as heat in all its divisions and sadness
somehow emanating from all the porous surfaces
of the non-existent world which is increasing inside
me and who am I and where am I headed for what
ports of tropical memory where brothers and sisters
each a hymn to the longest day and stars suddenly
come into view each with their unknown name
and I am lying there in a somewhere of jungles
and mountains consisting only of blue and heights
where gods are born out of overnight rock
the anticipation of something else I cannot define
maybe a friend whose birthday is half a year away
from mine and whom I have never met unless

that is why I have dreams and the continental shelf
becomes a thin pigment of greenish shale a lunation
embroidered with a memory that is not mine
so many similarities yet nothing holds a concatenation
of zeroes and conjectures and where planets strive
emptiness the emotions of the zodiac wild and evolving
until it is today again though only a few hours ago
talking to someone I don't remember who it was
large the commotion of vowels much like a tumbler
of gas and air and the reaches of glass so irreversible
I won't mind turning the page and the language
they speak on the non-existent world deep within me
it is my heart beating and something else which
requires a thermometer or a mounting gauge
at the door the multiple voices of a single person
what amazement to have been born and look !
the cancelled hands of the many who have tried
to climb but not succeeded the solar pyramid
so it is why the hour cannot proceed without itself
I am trying on new shoes for the errant way a path
that used to lead around the back to a porch where
fireflies are bottled by girls who have just become
it is pretty the way their hair and pinafores in the wind
blowzy sweetly daydreaming you know the way I am
this immense clarity this landspill these regions
widening into an albescent information about what
you may ask and the pigeons on the roof and kites
zigzagging into the month of august a part of the empire
each minute counts they say running out of print
the way I feel just now waking dry-mouthed I
wonder what it is I ache for wanting so much
to understand the dialect it is happening in the poem
it cannot be written how many were already published
in the non-existent world growing unconsciously
somewhere in the depths of my mind hemispheres

of unequal distances and a few colors too nightfall
with its yearning moon of aspirin and henna
consonant clusters not meant to be pronounced
and constantly this unyielding sadness to be
something vast and indefinable

clix

whose are these pronouns scattered in the grass ?
great black suns of ego ! portents of flashy idiom
languages unlearnt in a trice hypnotic elevator
shoes that move mysteriously through granite
and syntax of the void illusion and hospital
without birthright the naked little ones who ask
nothing of the gamma ray and the electric fish
that penetrate like needles the pharaonic eye
which of us will surrender first the envelope
of light and proceed into the aftermath of sleep
a conclusion to all the poetry of automobiles
to the hypotenuse and elision of afternoons spent
trading masks in the drugstore where fireflies
illumine the prescription desk for a brief hiatus
there are no more moments of self realization !
such as it is a new day offers its umbrellas to
fend off the enormous flares that devour time
you and I *yes* you and only I in search of the *other*
paradigms of vowel and subtraction of ciphers
situationism and circumflex accent the dialogue
between the republic and its autoincineration
how many times do we circle the same block
listening for car horns and the voice of glass
and adze a fiction of the ninth grade and heights
at the top of the only hotel permitted to Indra
god of brick and rain and we like ants cumulating
rice seeds and slender filaments of bamboo to

build our house of sound and ambition but what !
you and yes only I the undifferentiated equals
of the firestorm in the ear the impounded syllable
the unreason of living iota and omega shibboleth
you have worn my shoes for the last time !
madness intoxication & obsession for the *Form*
the disappearing waist the vise and shining clamp
the oracle ! the five thousand and fifty times
we exchanged glances and did not once recognize !
it was neither you nor I but the *other* in the grass

clx

as we go further north the zigzag becomes
less perfect the origin of things more questionable
and only when the horizontal line turns on itself
the snake with its tail in its mouth reciting in a
tufa-like oscan or umbrian the residues of a litany
do we begin to misunderstand there is no meaning
to the sounds rocks make to themselves and the echo
tripartite at the start then expanded to centimeters
of music with distance for a lyric are we disassembled
imagined divisions of a soul greater in parts than
its whole and booming voices antiphonies of waters
depthless as ink and fomented by warnings in shale
designs of sand lifted into the pyramidal air shaking
with childhood and sorrow and almost palpable
the memory of something happening in the mirror
shaving or electing to comb the unshorn grass a
mephitic poisoning the air with syllables of quanta
entire planets reduced to their opposites in inches
of spermatozoa gone mad we are born ! phrases
intelligible only to marble statuary on the brink
of reason of syllables rat-a-tat-tat in the imagery
of gods struggling to die ! and it is only for the leaves

we preserve speech and aphasia both and sleep stoned
in the illegitimate opium of myth becoming dissolved
in the outgoing and hands bereft of their others
a joint at a time do we then push out in caulked ships
from an Ionian shoreline breadth and width of sky
moving on the jagged edge of time a convex noise
a vowel with no pronunciation the end of space
in a thimble wreck and ruin of a single unsung note !
exhausted we fall back into a hieroglyphic detail
a portion only the effort to define in phonetics
an object perceived in a dream and which by dawn
vanishes in the enormous mirage of oblivion
as it is we step less and less sure into the day's
unpredictable chiaroscuro weather a knee at a time
emotions and shoulders and forgotten encomia
cities ! burrowed within ten thousand of them *we* !
flash and tinsel in the eye almost recognize the passenger
at our side the would-be cadaver of reflection
light-years away from the tear-duct and grief
that descend like a summer thunder storm by noon
and we are as ever scattered like atomic particles
in the numinous mountain-toppling winds
the head wound fever and careers of silence
fingers of delivery ! whispering seeds blowing
in a random cosmic accident

clxi

one over fifty !
the three worlds in dislocation as vedic demons
learning to yawn dissolve into cloud spirit
invisible in the thunderbolt that permeates all
rains and mountain-tops and dense woods
why did we ever come to this still place
stone and brick the dissensions of the soul

who will ever get back his life ? what of
the million summers the heat in bright
cycles the visions of immortality on the skin
the singing and praises the very innocence
of once and then the starless night blanketing
the whole and grief and distress and tears
everywhere looking for the body and its wounds
innumerable vulnerabilities sighing the recapped
versions of the only story possible from end
to beginning and from on high in secret balconies
goddesses wearing only silver anklets and
threats of an unhindered future the distant
vague demesne where mind travels when it
runs out of vowels and memory is put out to dry
what a vacation this has been ! sticks are counted
up to one over fifty and the child exhumed
to walk again in the sleep of planets and light
boundless the energies of a single watt and
batteries purchased in cheap basement stores
to last forever like all broken promises
when did we ever understand there is no remission
that the closing notes retain no echo
that air and the fundament of time are one
in the insanely brief instant of transformation
followed by endless unpunctuated silence

one over fifty !

clxii

Wednesday afternoon what did we know
of the end nothing but commas and the virtue
of an exclamation mark and pointless dots
extending separate infinities into the next room
where the charge-nurse languished in a wan light
planet mercury was ready to explode !

heat in its various quantities of meter and accent
circulating at quiet velocities no one noticed
a poetry being recited in hieroglyphic tones
ushering in the unexpected hour of a tin-plate sky
were those angels seraphim cherubim up there
operating the x-ray machine and buzzing
like outsize electric insects prepared to excavate
the despairing heart and take the trapped soul away
into what realms of oxided pillars and mists
a tomb at a time ! visuals of an alternate world
passing from hand to hand like old French postcards
a cathedral and history and the vacant cliffsides
of an empire unable to control its mountains and rivers
we are out of step with time ! legend and detritus
side by side litter the roadways and exits
a diesel engine purrs erratically though the night
and rain disintegrating rain corroding thought
and the puzzle of a mind dissolving in sadness
to remain ignorant ! to assume it is still yesterday !
yet to realize there is nothing in the sleeves
that Sanskrit can't be replaced by Italian
the figures great and small rotating eights !
the seas come and go and denizens of the deep
more eye than ear swarming into darkness
tender at birth more tender still in death
how is it so far away so fade so pallid the leaf
a sound meant to be indistinct a rumor in mulch
verb forms irregular and incomplete a phonetic
disarray for which no remedy exists a sun-spot
a blemish on the pellucid offering to the goddess
no wonder ! it keeps coming around small and
groundless the first and last vowel
in the syllabary of the rishis huddled and
praying in hospital waiting rooms and the *Gong !*
and corridors sliding from view and parking levels

forty stories high and the terrible final rush
Wednesday afternoon what did we know ?

clxiii
a lotus sutra

how many words does it take ? a valley
fills so easily with miles and lotuses
of five different hues where the god is hidden
an excursion by midafternoon to ruined cities
arcana epilogues and the voice made manifest
oracular and shapely in shimmering blooms
serenaded by swarms of bees and luscious
skies velvet azure opening up to the eye's
naked mind uncorrupted by language
effect of sound on meaning and the tensions
vibrating and enigmatic as to why we cannot
and the lexica of water and soul and registers
on a single note about the Buddha preaching
in the slums of Calcutta by day a smoking pipe
by night the revelations of all the afterworlds
broken promises shale nickel gravel cheap
basement store purchases if only we could
revive those we love if only by a magic wand
the hand would return to its original shape
and driving crazily over these Himalayan defiles
hallucinatory beings hitchhiking to see
the Dragon in full Tibetan head-dress kneeling
before an immense pagoda of ink-black hair
and gongs and bonzes and sutures in yellow
unraveling threads of pre-dynastic speech
statuary afloat three inches above earth
and moon-talk and goblins of red gas
careening in the head to be able to !
to arrive nowhere with nothing of value

haggling with lesser deities for a piece of silk
enduring insults in hill dialects come evening
incense consumed in fine blue mists sandalwood
aroma bliss the future at last cancelled
we can never of course and windows and
the machines that control doors and apses
asleep on our bamboo mats and the bus-driver
high above in the refined peaks of heaven
issuing instructions about the great Awakening

clxiv
DEVAVĀNĪPRAVEŚIKA*
saying it doesn't make it so months on
end the figment no less wavers a section
at a time carved out of infinity and still
steps up and down and the abyss here
just inches from the gasoline pump in
broad daylight and nobody really knows
discernment of so little value to offer fire
to the gods oblations of dried grass hues
autumnal and fading hills gathered dusk
obscurity words that issue out of stone
meaningless as sounds uttered in sleep
intrinsic nature of the universe hidden
in foolscap and drying ink a finger shapes
distance and longing afternoons in empty
schoolyards memory and ball playing echo
fists held up for five and junction coral
and hematite world spins out of control
the poets vie for voice to express and falter
each nothing more than a rote syllabary
of vowel and conjunct consonant rallied
against the fortunes of burning planets
and in front of the anthropology library

preaching until hoarse a bodhisattva
to remind that man is born of desire and
fruitless the lamps lit the waters poured
the structures built the cinema revolved
eyes and ears to the contrary mind is nothing
brick and mortar thistle and enigma
to sit staring in noisy cafes as students
who come and go in semesters of light
argue the exegesis of the Book and
pundits and slatterns and street peddlers
darkness wrapped around their knees
shoulders that learn to weep and plaint
sovereign thoughts destroyed by lust and
opium the perfumes that swell and nails
turning brown with anticipation of death

*(ENTRANCETOTHELANGUAGEOFTHEGODS)

clxv

canzone

with death's anticipation it repeats the solemn
afterword of time the inking spells that erase
and brooding nightmare in the moon's cold crease
a hellfire for a minute brighter gleams on earth
to imagine and forsake the endless rout a circle
and heat and rousing months no more than three
a summer's length abandoned in its listing sink
waters rise and gravid longing and tree-roots
that delve into memory's dark glen and mire
will withhold no more a grief and sorrowing
in fits that anchor clouds to their fierce speed
aloft hands that seem to fly in search of shape
a form to embrace the passing soul as it floats
ever up to planets mercurial and distant as
the sleeping boat itself that drifts vanishing afar

none hear the drowning roar the ancient sum
of sounds that once gave breath to leaf and voice
to statues made of dreams and did we too once
pass through this narrow path and gaze as if
to recognize in one another the incidental mask
the chance to touch and kiss and feel a warmth
a disguised mind a flowering thought that breaks
waking to the random lamp that lights a minute
then back to coils of night descends our names
that with it disappear into Persephone's sweet lap
petals plucked and evanescent hues that fade
all is as it never was a myth in stone and blade

clxvi

el paso

el paso just one step from the grave your pass
is not on my side your steps are out of touch
with mine the less you stand the more you fall
dust clouds and dusky skin and accents full
of illegal vowels and gun my shop and shoot
my hip and fling old glory aside the loss is big
you stand to die the more you swim from the
other side a legal move a movie in black and
thunder two swirls from my pistolero a glare
a consonant in double "s" and flight from mind
unreason for a simple fee an automatic weapon
and misunderstanding what better way to
sleep slipping one sky-folded belt into another
erasing mountains that filled the void before
we came to pass here in the grave-diggers lore
of old el paso you and me opposites of the same
brother front and back of a cardboard enemy
tossed from the saddle shot in the back given
a gunny sack for bed and nothing more to eat

stars fall on rushing diesels gelid moons rain
down on roaming hills in this western film
where we all play our flimsy shadow-roles
it's dun and dark and night has no end at last
& back in Rosa's cantina we can barely hear
the dying moan of a faded cowboy song

One little kiss and Felina good-bye

clxvii

what is due and what is past due
the ocher and the fade and the dun
that slope the hills of memory now gone
a storm of light in a thimble a glimpse
into what the heart can wear when all
is done sample of green in the dew
intransigent sky the above and beyond
what seeing can achieve a moment
of mercury a second of visitation
collapse the all in its slender reed
a wisp of hair the wind buys back and
rain that owns every Wednesday night
nothing sure in the lost hour nothing clean
that purifies the air of the gone breath
hesitation and prophesy in rust
the needle of direction dissolved in
its metal and the superfluous vowel
uttered when all have disappeared
what is left to say that the finger
has not already written in discard
a roaming in the grass a clutter of leaves
syllables of a vagrant sleep a tense
gone out of time in the great attempt
schoolyards fill with echoes and dust
feet and hands the tiniest shoulder

knees rubbed together to ignite a flame
between then and now impalpable
shadows that flit between scant thoughts
mind loosed from its captivity a balloon
of unspoken words escaping high
into the cloud-weft a volley of sounds
lament and plaint of dizzy earth
forever fall the distances
forever filled with grief

clxviii

Hiroshima , it's OK today's the day
we proved what ? what the brain of man
can do to solve the puzzle the quickest way
some grief up to the thousands the poison
sticks won't go away , Hiroshima
was too many years ago to care a stick
of dynamite a poke in the eye some
self-serving rhetoric the greatest in the world
this country owns up to its fabulous best
when ironing difficulties so nothing's left
what's the Japan, or for that matter
China too we're going back to the moon
where it's nice and cool and it's by far
the best seat to watch planet earth blow up
with no glaciers left to melt
no forests left to cultivate
a bare radioactive patch of dirt
Hiroshima , the future's ours to pay
and no children left to play

clxix

chiaroscuro days come and go the first
a last and in between all the fevers of a life

circumflex and grave the accents in our head
a depth to sorrow in graven stone a flower
from dust arisen a finger displayed in dew
and storms of light in a single eye to defy
whatever follows in its dark train the loud
a summer rain and clouds woven like thread
through porous rock the still-life painting
of the western slope the anticipation and
the dread of endless waiting rooms a flicker
up above a vowel extended for eternity a
something else we can't define a sentence
uttered thoughtlessly and x-rayed syllables
and medical chants repeated behind walls
so none can understand yet and yet we waver
if to stand is a mind's intent and to walk again
and explore for a brief while the small grass
protruding through cement and say to the *other*
who passes by undisguised a homeless soul
there is a truth somewhere in the air a vast
undeniable fiction that all that has ever been
a dream it was between you and me and born
and to die from the start no matter what
a hand held up to the infra-red and shapes
no sky has ever known and gods smaller
than lichen that clings to the now dead stump
alive ! it was when evening's dense curtain
folded the child in its soft breathless seams
the first a last and all the fevers of a life

clxx

who is that mythic being that lingers like a wave
on the thoughtless sea a voice tossed between
scant vowels a hand displaced between memories
hair taken by the wind to grottos in the sky

and like a lamp shining just once on the mystery
of a wall the shadows return to take it all
a sound beneath the optic nerve a cry outside
the sleeping ear some windows a door that
refuses to open a corridor down which drive
imaginary horses and their chariot so swift
a history without an alphabet a choir singing
without music and the noonday sun blackest
of the many stars that parade instantaneously
before turning their endless pages in the dark
who is that legendary entity that once appeared
on the shifting rock of time high above the quarrels
of grass and leaf the infinitely disguised reed that
played its momentary song of silence and retreat
a sorrow inches in diameter a grief like a stairwell
that goes down too deep and laments unheard that
pierce the office monotony with cries to turn back
because there is nothing to be done with mercury
when it reaches its planetary end and why do
the experts of colors that have no name pretend
life can resume its former contours and hues
if the calendar has no following day and light
contends with stone to find a place in space
to bed the one whose birthright has been denied
who is that mythic being that legendary entity
if not the child whose least step reached too far
whose bright hour was fixed in eternal sleep
if not the soul itself circling in flight at last ?

clxxi

the cut in the foil
there is nothing left to say
every vowel has come to its
final intransigent breath

nothing to write and re-word
nothing left to utter in stone and ply
no inks left to destroy order
no space left to imply disorder
the last poem has been unraveled
bee and ant and electric fish
pyramids juxtaposed to fireflies
a dish of toxic thought
a remnant of memory strung out to dry
on the high wire of temptation
that no mind can withstand
nothing left to discourse
a syllable of doom and light
a consonant lingering between echoes
of something that was never said
what walls that wonder wail
and sequences of never ending
the air and itself a small compass
that directs us nowhere
but to the end of thinking
circular and devastating
when there is nothing left to say
the written has been erased
and today greater than ever the sky
unmoored from man's puny noise
drifts into a greater Unknown
where sleep is freed
from waking

FINIS

Berkeley CA, 08-09-2019

**Poetry by Iván Argüelles
Published by
Luna Bisonte Prods:**

DIARIO DI UN OTTOGENARIO [2020]

TWILIGHT CANTOS [2019]

CIEN SONETOS [2018]

LAGARTO DE MI CORAZÓN [2018]

FRAGMENTS FROM A GONE WORLD [2017]

LA INTERRUPCIÓN CONVERSACIONAL [2016]

ORPHIC CANTOS [2015]

D U O P O E M A T A :
ILION—A TRANSCRIPTION
& ALTERTUMSWISSENSCHAFT [2015]

FIAT LUX [2014]

A DAY IN THE SUN [2012]

ULTERIOR VISIONS [2011]

All are available at:
https://www.lulu.com/spotlight/lunabisonteprods
or www.spdbooks.org

www.ingramcontent.com/pod-product-compliance
Lightning Source LLC
Chambersburg PA
CBHW031626160426
43196CB00006B/303